GETTING HITS

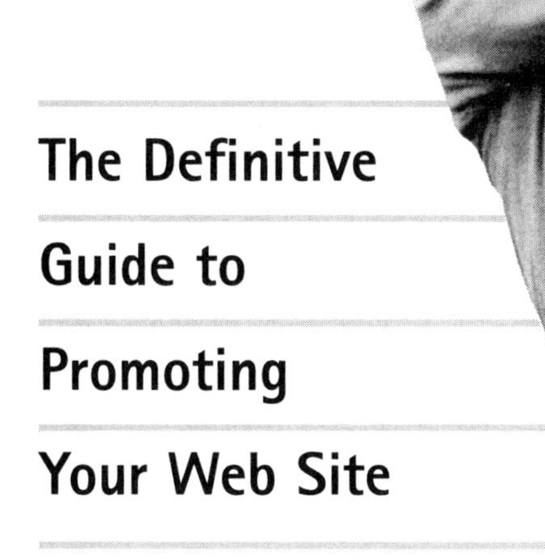

The Definitive Guide to Promoting Your Web Site

Don Sellers

Peachpit Press

GETTING HITS

Don Sellers

Peachpit Press
2414 Sixth Street
Berkeley, CA 94710
510-548-4393
800-283-9444
510-548-5991 (fax)

Find us on the World Wide Web at:
http://www.peachpit.com

Peachpit Press is a division of Addison Wesley Longman

Editor: Jeremy Judson
Copyeditor: Joseph Sadusky
Cover design: TMA Ted Mader + Associates
Interior design: Mimi Heft
Production: Margaret Copeland

Colophon
This book was created with QuarkXPress 3.32 on an 8100/80 PowerPC. The fonts used were Utopia and Rotis Sans, both from Adobe. It was printed on 50# Precision Smooth at Malloy Lithographing in Ann Arbor, MI.

ISBN 0-201-68815-8

9 8 7 6 5 4 3 2 1

Printed and bound in the United States of America

Dedicated to Steve Roth.
This book is just one of his many great ideas.

Table of Contents

FOREWORD

Three years ago you didn't need this book. Now you must have it. Take it from a NetGeezer.

I remember those simple days when the only place you announced a new World Wide Web site was the NCSA What's New page. It was an easier time to get attention. The Web was like a big trampoline, and jumping up and landing in one spot would create sympathetic waves everywhere else. It was also a time when the whole Internet would be down—yes, just essentially *off*—for a few hours at a time because of things that seem trivial today. It was simultaneously a very small world and one stretched very thin.

Then Yahoo and Netscape came along, and the small world suddenly got very crowded—and thick.

Hard as it is to believe, there was a time when we knew very little. Web site creators didn't know who was out there, how many people, what they wanted, or how to reach them. There were no search engines or indexes, just pages of hotlinks. At times, it seemed like *all* there were were pages of hotlinks. Oh, yes, and we had to walk uphill in both directions, clutching 10 miles of fiber optic cable.

Just as in the "virgin" forests of the American West, denizens and a landscape already existed on the Net, and the rush by average folks into the territory changed the ecology of the Net profoundly. However, unlike the original "pioneers," we could simply make more acreage, an option not available in the real world.

We were counting on folks to arrive in droves, starting with people who were like the very first early adopters who bought television sets. (According to the

Seattle Times, 6,000 families in Seattle had purchased televisions before any signals were being broadcast in the area—"Honey, let's gather round and watch the, uh, blank picture tube ....") Those of us who had gone ahead on the Net thought we had gone the adopters one better: everyone had computers and most folks had modems, so surely, if we built content, they would come.

Luckily for those of us who started businesses based on the Web, like the Web hosting and development company I co-founded in June 1994, we bet correctly; when the paradigm shifted sometime in 1995, and early adopters gave way to the merely technology aware, the battle for attention really began.

Churn and Chaff

In the space of a few months following Summer 1994, the Internet turned upside down; search engines, indexes, browsers, and other tools poured forth, and the commercial phase of the Web started up in earnest. Somewhere in there, I started the Internet Marketing Discussion List to try to put the business side of the Net into perspective.

Curious whether anyone really had the inside skinny, and eager to share perspectives with others in the same boat, I started the list in July 1994; within a week a thousand people subscribed, and it seemed like there might be a future in this Internet thing after all. The list was moderated, which meant that there was a chance of gleaning some wheat out of all the chaff.

The list endured for two years, until June 1996, when the weight of all the new users constantly pouring on the Net and onto the list—the foam of the churn, as it were—scared off the remaining veterans. The forum became an endless rerun of the same questions, as most Internet marketers had and have two primary concerns: announcing the site and generating a buzz from the launch, and keeping traffic returning.

What was terrific before the influx of new sites was that announcing and hyping were easy. Even when we transitioned from the NCSA What's New Page to multiple forums for finding and announcing sites, your site still got a tremendous boost from being listed in Yahoo. If you were lucky, Glenn Davis (now of Project Cool, www.projectcool.com) picked you as a Cool Site of the Day, and you suffered or enjoyed the "Death of 100,000 hits." You probably won't believe this now, but some sites—especially governmental—actually asked *not* to be named Cool Site, as they didn't have the bandwidth, staff, and equipment to handle it. As late as July 1995, one of our clients' appearance as a Cool Site generated 20 times the normal day's traffic.

The press was so highly focused on this "new" phenomenon that any reasonably savvy marketer could get a write-up (or ten), or at least get his or her URL mentioned all over the place. Back in January 1995, a *Forbes* writer called me up and asked me how you publicized a site—"besides getting quoted in this article," he added.

The maturation of the Net meant it was ever harder to really get the word out about a new site. You had to stand out from the background radiation, as hundreds and then thousands of new home pages and sites started up daily; you had to be as big or important as the major magazines, newspapers, software companies, and Internet content firms going online daily. In short, you had to become savvy.

Getting Hits is all about savvy. With the sheer volume of pages and sites on the Internet, unless you're IBM or Time-Warner, you have to use smarts to get your site noticed, not bulk mail. Simple things like maximizing the effectiveness of your signature line in e-mail; targeting your Web ads and finding the right destination for them; or even just learning how to get listed correctly and fully in Web search engines can push you into the awareness of ten or a hundred times the users you would have had. Or, better yet, than your competitor is getting.

People have asked me over the last several months for a book that will address these issues and give them the ability to stand out from the crowd. Now, in *Getting Hits*, I have it— and so do you. This book will make you clever.

Glenn Fleishman
Catalog Manager
Amazon.com, Inc.
Seattle, Washington

PREFACE

Perhaps the only certainty about the Web is that it will change, and change rapidly. If you spend much time online you soon realize that you're witnessing a vibrant evolution—one that mutates so rapidly it outstrips the capacities of those who would strive to monitor it. The best method of attempting to stay ahead of Web developments is to observe the Web itself, perhaps supplementing your research with facts garnered from other forms of electronic media. Printed media, such as books, magazines, and newsletters just can't keep up.

So why write a book about Web site promotion (or perhaps more importantly, why buy one)? There are a number of good reasons. Although some of the material in *Getting Hits* can also be found on the Web, it is not an easy job to ferret it out. The greatest strength of the Web, the staggering number of sites that can all be accessed with equal ease, is also its biggest handicap; such an enormous multitude of sites makes finding dispersed specialized information very difficult. The true nuggets of Web site promotion can be found scattered all over the place; some lies buried deep within Web pages, but some reside only in the minds of those experts knowledgeable in the ways of attracting visitors to sites. I searched everywhere—on line, off line, through published material and personal interviews. The information I found was often contradictory, and its validity needed to be tested. Once I had done this, I analyzed and ordered the results: the outcome of all of this labor is *Getting Hits*. I wanted to gather all the best information in one compact, easy-to-use form.

Getting Hits is the book that I searched for when I decided to promote my Web site. I wanted a book that would provide the knowledge to increase the numbers of visitors to my site by employing the entire spectrum of Web site promotion techniques such as search engine results, site linking, working newsgroups and mailing lists, and working the off-line media. In addition, I wanted a book that would give me the inside scoop about Web advertising: where the bargains were, how to design and launch an effective Web campaign, how to evaluate hit reports from my point-of-presence provider, and how to fine tune my campaign for maximum return on investment. No such book existed, but now, in *Getting Hits*, one does.

How to be seen. That's what *Getting Hits* is all about.

Who's Hitting What

One of the first steps you must take when you plan a Web site promotion campaign is to define your target audience (see "Your Target Audience" in Chapter 1, *A Million Ways to Get Hits*). Your target audience comprises part of that great, difficult-to-analyze mass of citizens who populate the Internet: the netizens. Who are the netizens? What sites are they visiting?

When I pondered writing a summary of who is hitting what on the Web, I considered having the entire section just say this: "Launch your Web browser. Go to CyberAtlas `http://www.cyberatlas.com`, NPD Group `http://pcmeter.com`, and Georgia Tech's WWW Users Survey `http://www.cc.gatech.edu/gvu/user_surveys`. Have a ball."

And that would be it. If you want to be on top of the Web you have to know what's happening now, and you can get fairly current Web statistics from those sites. The Web changes so rapidly that right now was really just a moment ago: anything published as current knowledge is really a snapshot of recent history. But a snapshot, even one that's necessarily out of date, can provide a starting point. And a series of snapshots can indicate movement and direction.

Internet statistical gathering may still be in its infancy, but it's evolving rapidly and showing signs of someday being quite well developed. In many ways the Internet lends itself to demographic analysis, in other ways it resists it. Studies differ in methodology and sometimes disagree radically in results. However, the need for marketers to have solid, reliable demographics has fueled an increasing understanding of who is online and where the netizens are going, so more is known now that was as little as a year ago.

Who's At Bat

In this section I will look at recent history; in the next section, "Who's On Deck," I'll look at trends and forecasts.

Netizens are young. One-tenth of American Internet users are children; more than half of those Americans who access the Web are between the ages of 16 and 34.

Netizens are numerous, but census data conflicts appreciably. In mid 1996, Intelliquest `http://www.intelliquest.com` released a survey that showed 35 million Americans over the age of 16 had been on line at least once during a three-month period. But most of those were short-lived visitors; only 13.8 million had been on line more than five hours a week. Other studies put the number of Americans on line at as low as 10 million for the same approximate period.

Netizens are intelligent. According to Nielsen Media Research `http://www.nielsenmedia.com`, 64% have some type of college degree. Intelliquest `http://www.intelliquest.com` found that 61% labeled themselves avid readers, versus 47% of the general population.

Netizens are wealthy. A number of studies have found the median income of Internet users to be about $60,000 per year. One-quarter of Web users have a yearly income of more than $80,000.

Netizens are pretty similar. The vast majority of on-line Americans are white. Two-thirds are male. Most netizens access the Internet from home.

However, in some ways, netizens are diverse. Half of on-line Americans are married and half are not. A CommerceNet and Nielsen Media Research `http://www.nielsenmedia.com` study showed that people varied in their Net usage—about 15% of Internet users accounted for 50% of usage.

Netizens visit the same sites. PC Meter reported that 65% of home users used search engines in mid 1996, most visiting a few popular search engine sites. Recent top news, information, and entertainment sites were: ZD Net `zdnet.com`, MSNBC `msnbc.com`, Pathfinder `pathfinder.com`, NBC `nbc.com`, and c|net `cnet.com`.

The Net is growing. The number of hosts (reachable computers) connected to the Internet has been growing at an average of 97% a year for the past several years.

Who's On Deck

Some on-line trends couldn't be more obvious. Others look probable, but since rapid change seems to be one of the Internet's basic hallmarks, one should remain skeptical. Here's what the crystal ball says.

The numbers of netizens will continue to grow, but the pace may slacken. Two studies predict an average of of 160 million Internet users by 1999.

On-line demographics will continue to move toward reflecting the general population because of decreased cost and increased awareness and utility. American netizens will include increasing numbers of minorities, women, and older
people.

More netizens will access the Web from ISPs (Internet Service Providers). Coopers & Lybrand Consulting found that ISPs were growing faster than traditional on-line services such as America Online and CompuServe. That trend will probably continue, especially when telephone and cable companies begin to penetrate the on-line access market.

In addition to trends regarding netizens, it is possible to make a few predictions regarding the Web itself.

The Web has been volatile and will remain so for some time. New sites will be able to gain popularity very quickly.

Marketing on the Web will explode. Hambrecht & Quist `http://www.hamquist.com/research/stats/internet.html` predicts that by the year 2000, on-line entertainment, information, and shopping will take in $10 billion a year. A Forrester Research `http://www.forrester.com` study showed that the current $500 million in sales on the Internet will become $6.6 billion by the year 2000.

Today's Program

Now that you have an idea of the vast pool from which you will draw your potential visitors, how do you get them into your site? The Web represents a totally new paradigm in commerce and must be visualized in a new way.

The paradigm I use when imagining the Web is that of hundreds of thousands of stores orbiting in space. To get to a store, you teleport into it. You look around, see if you like it, and, if not, teleport out. To go to another store, many stores offer you the convenience of lots of teleport booths (links out to other sites) ringing their main rooms. In fact, some stores, like search engines, only offer custom teleport booths. You go to the search store, ask for an assortment of teleporters to a particular kind of place, and they will deliver those links to you. All they ask is that they can display some advertising while you are waiting.

Some stores hide their teleport links in a dusty room at the back of the basement. Some stores don't provide any teleporters out, and you have to use your hand-held teleporter to go to some favorite site you've been to before or have heard about.

That's the Web: millions of people teleporting into and out of hundreds of thousands of stores. How do you get them to visit your store, that is, to hit your site? It seems an impossible, overwhelming task. But it's a task that people accomplish every day, with a combination of diligence and the insights and knowledge necessary for getting hits.

Approach of Book

My goal in writing *Getting Hits* was to create a pragmatic, solution-based handbook that anyone could use to increase traffic on a Web site. I begin with an overview of the different methods you can use to increase hits and then step through them one by one. I lay the groundwork for a promotional campaign and investigate the different opportunities in publicity (promoting for free) and advertising (promoting for money). Because the Web changes so rapidly, wherever possible I have highlighted Web source sites and other on-line resources like this: `http://www.cyberatlas.com`. Use these resources to keep up with what's happening today.

Pinch Hitters

Very few books can be written alone, and *Getting Hits* was no exception. I sought the help, counsel, and knowledge of a number of individuals to create this work. Glenn Fleishman, Web marketing master, not only lent his critical insights throughout the writing process, but he generously wrote the Foreword and made a technical edit of the book. Steve Roth, who had the original idea for the book, reviewed material and provided direction. David Blatner and Ole Kvern supplied their usual calm moral support.

Because the Web changes so quickly, Peachpit Press and I wanted to make the book as timely as possible and publish it promptly so it would accurately reflect the current state of the Web. I realized I couldn't accomplish that goal and maintain high quality if I tried to write the book alone, so I drafted some other players for my team to write some of the chapters. I was fortunate to recruit these particular pinch hitters into my dugout; they are experts in their fields and skilled writers to boot.

John Schick

John Schick wrote Chapter 8, *Advertising Overview*; Chapter 9, *Launching Your Web Ad Campaign*; and Chapter 10, *Refining Your Web Ad Campaign*. John is President of SI Software, Chicago, IL `http://www.sisoftware.com`, and is an Internet consultant and software developer specializing in Web advertising, marketing, and promotion. John holds an M.B.A. in marketing from Loyola University of Chicago. Previously, John was V.P. of Marketing for an *INC.* 500 “fastest growing” technology company. He has helped launch numerous U.S., Canadian, and U.K. software ventures.

Jeff Carlson

Jeff Carlson wrote Chapter 4, *How to Get Quality Links*, and Chapter 5, *How to Get Links from Hundreds of Sites*. Jeff’s a switch hitter, and can play just about any position on the Web field, from designing sites to editing fiction. Jeff is Editor of eSCENE, The World's Best Online Fiction `http://www.etext.org/Zines/eScene`; his company, Never Enough Coffee creations `http://www.halcyon.com/kepi`, specializes in Web design, writing, editing, and illustration. Jeff also works as a freelance writer and editor, with articles appearing most recently in Adobe.mag `http://www.adobemag.com`. He holds a B.A. in English Writing from Whitworth College.

1

A Million Ways to Get Hits

Each time a server—the "sender" of information on a computer network—acts to pass something to a Web browser—the receiver of this information—it counts as a hit. This "something" can be the text of a page, or an illustration, or a File Not Found error message. A Web page can be composed of any number of the "somethings"; as a result, hits can be viewed as indications of server activity, but little else. Ten hits on the same server could mean that ten browsers have been sent ten single-file Web pages, or that one browser has been sent one Web page that includes nine files. The indistinct nature of the term hit has caused it to fall into disfavor by those who passionately care about how many visitors arrive at Web sites. Terms like "impression" or "view" or "visit" make much more sense when one attempts to measure how many people come to a Web site and what features they look into while they are there.

But since you've picked up this book, you probably have an idea in the back of your mind that hits are good. And so they are. Like the number of nibbles you have while fishing or the number of dollar bills in your wallet, more—more often than not—is better. Hits act as an imprecise indication that people are visiting your site.

You have a site because you want visitors. You may have built a commercial site hoping to corner the market in mail order sales to herb gardeners, or an association's site providing information and links to home brewers, or a personal page to let the world know that you exist (and that you have a weakness for Camille Saint-Saëns and Australian sheep dogs). Whatever kind of site you've built, once you build it you can sit back and visitors will come. But probably not very many. To draw visitors to your site you must promote it, through publicity (which you don't pay for) or advertising (which you do).

SEARCH ENGINE SEMANTICS

I refer to the Web's general search tools as "search engines." Speaking precisely, a search engine is a set of computer instructions that asks you to input what you are looking for and then searches through some data for it. In many word processors, a search engine known as the Find command scans a file for a word or a phrase and highlights it for you. All popular Web site locators use search engines as a critical part of their interface, and hence Net surfers generally use the term "search engine" when referring to them as a class.

There are literally a million ways to get hits, or attract people to your site. People will come to you via a staggering variety of visit triggers: links, referrals, postings, whispered conversations around the office water cooler. However, most visitors arrive from other locations on the Web. Some visit triggers, like search engines, produce the bulk of visitors for many sites. Other visit triggers, like Usenet newsgroups, may be critical to the success of one site while totally irrelevant to the popularity of another. The vast number of triggers and their diversity helps make the process of attracting people to your Web site more of an art than a science. To be productive, you must tailor your campaign to your particular site and to the audience that you wish to draw.

As you formulate your Web promotion effort you must understand the ins and outs of the different visit triggers so you can build your campaign effectively. First, you need to familiarize yourself with the search engines. Then you must understand the various opportunities on- and offline for publicizing your site. Third, you need to become expert in the rapidly changing area of Web advertising. Once you are armed with this information, you are ready to prepare promotion, taking into account the logistics of your site and your target audience as well.

Search Engines

Probably the single most important step you can take to attract visitors to your site is to understand search engines and how they can help potential visitors find you. Most people familiar with the Web have used search engines—those sites where you type in a term like "peanuts," click on a search button, and sit back while the search engine spits out page after page of links to sites that somehow have something to do with peanuts (although often one can't immediately see the connection).

If you've spent any time using search engines, you've probably realized that they all seem to work differently. Some of them, like Yahoo `http://www.yahoo.com`, organize their data in hierarchical subject categories. Other search engines that appear superficially equivalent will yield different results when searching for the same terms. The difference boils down to the various ways that these sites acquire, store, categorize, and search through their data.

As a site promoter you want your site to appear in the first ten links delivered by a search engine. I devote two chapters to that process: Chapter 2, *How Search Engines Think*, and Chapter 3, *Making Search Engines Do Your Bidding*. To give you some background, I'll first discuss the three general classifications of search engines: spider indexes, general directories, and hermaphrodites.

Spider Indexes

Spiders, also known as crawlers, automatically search the Web for pages. Like little electronic robots, they putter around, scanning sites, following links, and sending back information on the site to their mother database. Many of the most popular search engines use spiders to gather information and then store the data as an index, hence the term spider index.

Most Web surfers have used spider indexes like Alta Vista `http://www.altavista.digital.com` or Lycos `http://www.lycos.com`. Spider indexes pack a lot of wallop: their databases can hold vast amounts of information on the Net (some keep tabs on over 50 million pages). Because they update automatically, spider indexes can maintain fairly timely databases: some have contents that may be at the most a few weeks out of date. On the other hand, because spider indexes tend to check out a great amount of material, and because they categorize their databases in a fairly unsophisticated manner, one may be overwhelmed with search results that don't jive with what one is really looking for. Spider indexes' thoroughness provides a plus for you as a site creator: a spider may find your site even if you do nothing to promote it. However, all major spider indexes allow you to submit your site to them so they will be sure to include it in their database.

General Directories

Directories abound on the Web, but most of them deal with specific subjects such as the best places to shop or the restaurants available in a particular location. Only a few directories, which I call general directories, have attempted to include the full breadth of material available on the Web. General directories, the most famous of which is Yahoo, differ from spider indexes in two important ways. First, general directories principally rely on submissions from the site creators for the sites that they include. Second, general directories employ people to compile their sites into subject-based hierarchical categories. The top categories are general, whereas subcategories become more and more specific until you find what you are looking for. For example, if you look for Yahoo's link to the Seattle Mariners you will find it under Regional:U.S. States:Washington:Cities: Seattle:Recreation and Sports:Sports:Seattle Mariners.

General directories often yield good results when searching for a Web site. You can dig through a general directory logically, category by category, sometimes uncovering links you might otherwise miss. When you are using its search engine, a directory may well prove more effective than an index, because a directory can produce pages related conceptually, even if they use different words for the same concept (for example, if one page uses the term "hitter" and the other uses "slugger").

The fact that a site creator must apply to a general directory for inclusion acts to filter out sites that don't want visitors or don't know how to get them. Because directories rely on human input, their contents may be more out of date than a spider index's. In addition, a search through a directory may miss a link if you look for it in the wrong place. That's one of the reasons that the best general directories, like Yahoo, include a search engine to help you sift through their contents.

Hermaphrodites

Excite `http://www.excite.com` represents the first example of employing computer technology to meld the strengths of spider indexes and general directories. Excite uses a spider to scan millions of Web pages, creating its database. Then Excite performs an artificial-intelligence-based statistical analysis of each Web page, looking for word proximity and cataloging similar results together in its internally created directory. Excite describes the process as determining the "dominant themes" for a page. When someone searches Excite for terms similar to the dominant theme, that category is delivered.

Excite's hermaphroditic technology enables it to gather a giant database with spiders, while enabling the user to find material that is conceptually related. In practice, Excite often produces uncannily good results, although occasionally this search tool misses the mark completely.

Links

Sometimes a search will be much more successful if carried out from one of a wide variety of links sites rather than from a search engine. Some links sites target particular subjects. Others provide links to sites of a particular quality.

The use of hyperlinks probably does more than any other feature to separate the World Wide Web from other communication media. Links (including those from search engines) represent the most common trigger by far for sending someone to your Web site. In the early days of the Web, many site owners believed the way to get the most visits was to get as many links as possible. Now experience has shown that a single linking page with the proper characteristics and popularity can produce substantially more visits than links from hundreds of sites in Web Siberia. The key to establishing links is to go for quality first and quantity second.

Some pages on the Web contain links and little else, while others may only provide a few links sprinkled among a sea of information. These links pages exist in a spectrum, starting with large directories covering multiple subjects, through specialty sites that provide a variety of information on a single subject, to pages that only contain links. Pages with links can also be classified in these two ways: those containing links to particular subjects, or those with links to sites of a particular (usually high) quality. I discuss the sites that are more likely to produce quality hits in Chapter 4, *How to Get Quality Links*, and the what-the-hell let's-cast-a-wide-net sites in Chapter 5, *How to Get Links from Hundreds of Sites*.

Sites of Related Interest

Your passion has always been the history of minor league baseball, so you've decided to launch a Web site with your volumes of research on the subject. But now that you've built it, who will come? Baseball nuts, that's who, and they flock to the baseball-related sites of the Web. You may be able to establish links from a content site that covers a particular baseball subject, or from directory or links pages that cover baseball in general.

Content Sites

Do any sites exist which have similar or related content to yours? The answer is often yes. In this case, you'd probably want to begin with the official site of The National Association of Professional Baseball Leagues, "Where It All Begins" `http://www.minorleaguebaseball.com/`. Or you could try to get a link from the site of a minor league ball club, like the Wilmington Blue Rocks `http://www.bluerocks.com/` in the Carolina league.

Your site has to pertain to a pretty obscure subject before you will be unable to find sites of similar content. Most content sites will want to evaluate the quality of your site and the appropriateness of providing a link to it before they go ahead and do so. Sometimes internal policy will dictate what kinds of sites they can link to.

Directories and Links Pages

Sites that will often gladly link to yours will be directories and links pages. These sites make it their business to be comprehensive in their links to sites of a particular subject. Baseball Directory of America's Sports Headquarters `http://sport-hq.com/spectate/baseball/baseball.shtml` provides a large directory of baseball related sites (see Figure 1-1). The directory is sufficiently large to warrant the inclusion of a search engine.

ASHQ Search | Reset

☒ Spectate ☐ Outdoor ☐ Recreation

BASEBALL DIRECTORY

- **Major League**
  - Ballparks/Stadiums
  - Fantasy
  - Gambling & Wagering
  - Information Services
  - Memorabilia, Collectibles & Trading Cards
  - Merchandise
  - News Groups & Chat Rooms
  - Players/Managers/Personalites
  - Scores, Schedules & Stats
  - **Teams**
    - American League
    - National League
    - Expansion
  - Other MLB Sites
- **Minor Leagues**
  - Information Services
  - Leagues
  - News Groups & Chat Rooms
  - Scores, Schedules & Stats
  - Teams
- **International**
  - Information Services
  - Leagues
  - News Groups & Chat Rooms
  - Scores, Schedules & Stats
  - Teams

Figure 1–1 The Baseball Directory of the America's Sports Headquarters site.

Likewise, John Skilton's BASEBALL LINKS `http://www.pc-professor.com/baseball/`, which professes to be a links site, is so large ("If you can't find what you're looking for, it probably doesn't exist yet on the Internet") that it has a directory-like structure to help you navigate to its pages of links (see Figure 1-2).

American Association (Class AAA)

League Sites

- American Association - FanLink
- American Association - Minor League Baseball

Team Sites

- Buffalo Bisons - WGR News Radio
- Buffalo Bisons - Minor League Baseball
- Indianapolis Indians - Minor League Baseball
- Indianapolis Indians - WRTV
- Iowa Cubs - Official Site
- Iowa Cubs - Minor League Baseball
- Louisville Redbirds - Minor League Baseball
- Nashville Sounds - Cari Bloodworth
- Nashville Sounds - Minor League Baseball
- New Orleans Zephyrs - Paul Johnstone/Terence Folan
- New Orleans Zephyrs - Minor League Baseball
- New Orleans Zephyrs - Official Site
- Oklahoma City 89ers - Keystone Technology
- Oklahoma City 89ers - Minor League Baseball

Figure 1-2 Part of a links page on John Skilton's BASEBALL LINKS.

Awards Sites

The egalitarian nature of the Web and its rapid growth have led to another form of aid to help surfers discover Web sites: the award site. The genesis of this concept was the Cool Site of the Day, which every day offered a different Web site of particular quality or interest and could have an enormous impact on the popularity of a site. This has led to directories that rate sites by quality, becoming directories of award sites. Getting an award site to notice you can be tricky, but is often worth the effort.

If you took a look at John Skilton's BASEBALL LINKS `http://www.pc-professor.com/baseball/`, you may have noticed his long list of awards. He has received awards for general high quality, like Blue Planet's Cool Site of the Day, and awards from sites that only deal with sports, like the Awesome Sports Site of the Month.

Announce Sites

Some sites just exist to announce that other sites exist. Sounds weird, doesn't it? The dynamic and massive nature of the Web has made announce sites a popular way for surfers to know what's new. Announce sites such as What's New Too `http://newtoo.manifest.com` list over 500 new Web sites a day. Many people find announce sites entertaining just because of the mind-boggling breadth of sites that appear. (Such people also have a taste for random site generators.) You can submit your site to announce sites easily; in fact, services exist that will submit your site to many announce sites for free.

Newsgroups & Mailing Lists

Newsgroups and mailing lists represent two methods of communication that were distributed by the Internet (and other networks) long before the World Wide Web appeared. Both newsgroups and mailing lists can provide a valuable resource for publicizing a Web site, because their readers are actively engaged in discussing particular subjects (like minor league baseball). Newsgroups and mailing lists comprise communities of people who know each other. A stranger, especially one promoting a Web site, needs to treat these venerable (and sometimes touchy) institutions with the respect and consideration they're due. I discuss the delicate but often valuable process of promoting to newsgroups and mailing lists in Chapter 6, *Mining the Hidden Gold in Mailing Lists and Newsgroups*.

Newsgroups

One of the perplexing aspects of newsgroups is that most Net surfers find it impossible to describe exactly what newsgroups are. From a casual user's perspective, newsgroups appear to be discussion groups or exchanges of information that relate to the hierarchical name of the group (for example, rec.sport.baseball). More than 8,000 newsgroups (see Figure 1-3) comprise Usenet, which is distributed on networks all over the world. These days, most Web surfers access newsgroups through their service provider, which actually subscribes to the newsgroups. However, many providers will take a pass on newsgroups whose content they find too unseemly or too obscure to be popular.

Mailing Lists

Mailing lists represent e-mail equivalent of newsgroups. After subscribing to the list, you receive e-mail messages that people post to the list. Of course, you can

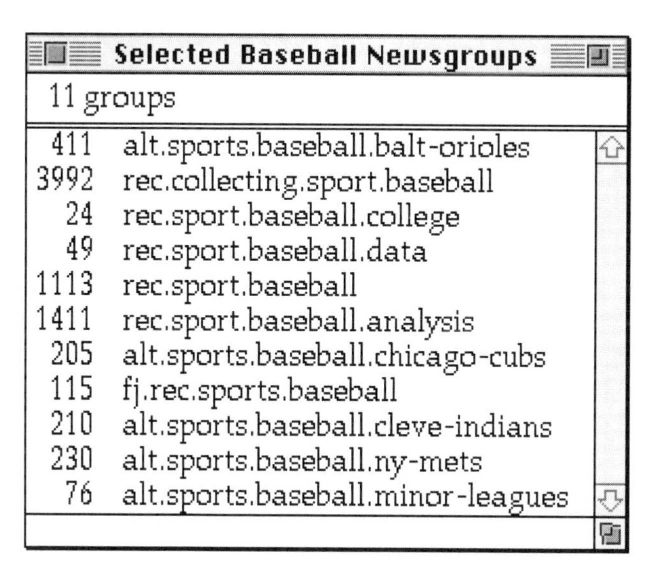

Figure 1–3 The mind-boggling diversity of newsgroups.

post to the list, too. Over 40,000 mailing lists exist, so you will likely find at least one list that has the appropriate subject for your announcement. For example, the mailing list *minors-scores* states as its purpose the discussion of all important issues affecting minor league baseball. Most mailing lists will accept anyone as a member, while some restrict their membership to people who can make valuable contributions to the discussion.

Media

Any good publicist owns a card file (or an electronic equivalent) bulging with the names of writers, editors, reviewers, producers, and publishers; that's especially true of those who publicize on the Web. The Web teems with the electronic equivalent of magazines, newsletters, and other publications. Some of these publications only exist online, while others draw material and support from off-line parent publications.

In the off-line world, general-readership print publications have become much less likely than they once were to carry stories about particular sites, unless there's a hook. But targeted print media can be a valuable source of hits.

On-line

Electronic media vary widely in purpose and content. Popular web magazines, newspapers, and news sites such as Interactive HotWired, Age Digital, and c|net keep abreast of what's new and notable on the net. Other e-zines target specific subject matter. The Web-related media provide ample opportunities for links that thousands will follow to your site. I discuss how to effectively work with the on-line media in Chapter 4, *How to Get Quality Links*.

Off-line

A number of different strategies can be taken to promote your site off-line. First, there exist a number of magazines, books, and directories that will list Web sites. Some of these publications attempt to include as many sites as possible, while others need to be approached correctly to produce positive results. People promoting Web sites often forget about publications that target the same subject matter as their site contains. A brief mention in a column in the right magazine could produce thousands of visits to your site.

Site promoters often miss an opportunity that's right in front of them: the paper that they generate in their business every day. Stationery, business cards, marketing material, and press releases all provide opportunities for promoting a site. I delve into the intricacies of working the off-line media in Chapter 7, *Producing Hits Offline*.

Advertising

Advertising, still in its infancy on the Web, has become such an important vehicle in Web site promotion that I devote an entire section to it. The dollars spent on Web advertising have been exploding, most recently doubling from the last quarter of 1995 to the first quarter of 1996, when they totaled about $26 million. Over 60 percent of that amount was spent at just ten popular sites.

Most Web advertising consists of your paying for the placement of graphic billboards (called banners) on someone else's site that are hyperlinked back to your site. You can look at it as an evolution of a basic link, but in this case the advertiser gets to decide what will grab the browser's eye, and pays for the privilege. I discuss the history and basics of Web advertising in Chapter 8, *Advertising Overview*.

Successful Web advertising requires a well-thought-out campaign that includes your site, your message and your ad placement, which you test and rework until you get it right.

The Paid Attraction

Often the planning of a Web campaign becomes the time for much soul-searching about your site. When you begin to consider paying for the opportunity of attracting visitors, you begin to realize you must be crystal-clear about your site's design, who you want to draw to it, and what advertising message you will use to lure them. Then you need to design a number of different banners that you hope will produce the most click-throughs (arrivals at your site from banner clicks), and then prepare to test, test, and test again to find the best banner and venues for your campaign.

I discuss these aspects of Web advertising in Chapter 9, *Launching Your Web Ad Campaign*, along with the next step in the process: buying advertising on the Web. Web advertising rates vary widely, and bargains exist if you know how to look for them. You need to understand the ins and outs of standard advertising contracts, how to buy keywords on search engine sites, and how to barter for advertising.

Refining the Ad Campaign

To be most cost-effective, a Web advertising campaign has to be a dynamic process with testing, evaluating, fine tuning, and maintenance. To test a campaign adequately, you need the appropriate server reports from your point-of-presence provider, andyou must interpret them correctly. Banners, keywords, and advertising sites must all be evaluated for their return on your investment. Your site needs to provide impetus to keep visitors returning, possibly by using entertainment, changing information, or giveaways. I discuss the best ways to produce the best results in Chapter 10, *Refining Your Web Ad Campaign*.

Your Site

This may seem silly, but one of the most common mistakes that people make is starting to promote a Web site before it's finished. Is your site ready not only to receive visitors but to make them want to come back? This book cannot attempt to deliver a course in effective Web page design. But here are a few tips to make sure you are on the right track.

Home Page

Is your home page friendly, accessible, easy to understand? Does it effectively communicate the message, subject, and tone of your entire site? Does it display clear navigational links to the main areas of your site? Does it give the viewer an opportunity to send feedback to you? If not, seriously consider working on refining the site before starting the campaign.

Page Size

What's the file size (including graphics) of your pages, especially your home page and those linked directly to it? Is it over 60K? A 60K file takes about a minute to download with a 14.4 modem and so is considered the maximum limit for a Web page. For the same reasons, seriously consider the download time of more recent innovations such as frames, sound, and video. Do they enhance the site sufficiently to make the wait worthwhile?

Geography

Are your site's pages linked one after another after another and so on? Such a vertical layout makes navigation tedious. The same is true of a horizontal layout, where too many individual pages are linked directly to your home page. Sites with easy navigation often display a grid pattern. For example, a site with five category pages linked to the home page with four pages linked vertically under each category page provides easy access. Of course, not all sites will lend themselves to this approach, but you should seriously consider your site's ease of navigation before you invite people in.

Your Target Audience

Who do you want to come to your site? Anybody at all? Usually, Web sites are most effective when they know who they want to host. Moreover, the nature of your audience becomes critical when you begin your promotion. You need to categorize your intended audience by age, gender, income, and interests before your begin.

Your Promotional Package

In the course of your promotional effort you will send information to search engines, site administrators, journalists, newsgroups, and others. This task can be made easier if you take some time to think about, prepare, and refine the following promotional material. Type this information into a word processing program that will allow you to copy blocks of the text, so you can paste it into forms and letters.

Title

Your site's title should not only catch people's attention, it should also convey the essence of your site.

URL

Before you've typed your URL (and pasted it into your browser's Open Location dialog box to test it), you should consider whether your URL will be stable for some time.

Contact Information

Your name, e-mail address, phone and fax number should be here, ready for copying and pasting.

Keywords

You will need about ten keywords for search engines that will match the queries of people searching for your site.

Description

It will be handy to have four descriptions of your site in the following lengths: one sentence, 25 words, 50 words, and 75 words.

Here's an example of each.

> One sentence:
>
> *Baseball Nut provides the most comprehensive resource on all things baseball—past, present, and future.*
>
> 25 words:
>
> *Baseball Nut must be cracked! No other web site worships baseball so devoutly as this comprehensive resource on the world's greatest and best-loved game!*
>
> 50 words:
>
> *Baseball Nut must be cracked! No other web site worships baseball so devoutly as this comprehensive resource on the world's greatest game! Latest scores? Sure! But Baseball Nut offers much, much more: profiles, statistics, features, history, and trivia on everything baseball from pitching speeds to baseball stamps to players' salaries.*

75 words:

Baseball Nut must be cracked! No other web site worships baseball so devoutly and fervently as this comprehensive resource on the world's greatest game! Latest scores? Current dugout chatter? Late breaking news? Of course! But Baseball Nut offers much, much more: profiles, statistics, features, history, and trivia on everything baseball from pitching speeds to baseball stamps to players' salaries. Watch for giveaways and contests like a chance to win a trip to the World Series!

Press Release

Develop a 500–1000 word press release that can act as the principal source of information for a newsbite or short article. A press release needs to be straightforward but interesting, written in a manner that will be accessible to a lay reader with little or no knowledge about the Web or the subject of your site. In order to give the journalist meat to work with, make the press release a self-contained piece, concentrating on the what, where, why, and who of your site. Try to include quotes, if appropriate. And be sure to include the site title, the URL, and the contact person information.

The following is a sample press release.

FOR IMMEDIATE RELEASE

January 15, 1997

BASEBALL NUT UNVEILS NEW WEB SITE

Cooperstown, NY—The Baseball Nut today swings for the wall by unveiling a new World Wide Web site that provides the Web's most comprehensive resource on all things baseball—past, present, and future.

The new site, Baseball Nut (http://www.baseballnut.com) has been designed for accessibility, allowing information to be found quickly and easily. All of the site's 400-plus pages have been optimized for rapid display and easy scanning. Prominent links between pages have been designed and tested to provide the most intuitive means of navigating through the large site.

"Our goal was to make the make the site as easy to channel surf as your cable TV," said Ron Alexander, vice-president - site engineering. "We want our visitors to be part of an engaging, entertaining experience, free from mental discomfort produced by slow display times and clumsy, non-intuitive navigational aids."

Baseball Nut has been designed for flexibility: discussion areas, scores, and statistics will be updated continuously. Other areas will be renewed and revised on an as needed basis—often several times a day.

"We see ourselves as a real-time communication medium," said Ron Alexander. "The same information a fan receives from a radio, newspaper, scorecard, encyclopedia, or sports bar discussion can all be easily obtained from the site."

Baseball Nut contains six main areas:

* Current News, Scores, and Statistics
* History of the Game
* Features and Profiles
* Dugout Discussion
* Fan Madness
* Trivia

The Trivia section has been built around regularly scheduled promotions and contests, and features a yearly sweepstakes which will have as its Grand Prize a trip for four to all games of the World Series.

Baseball Nut has been designed to satisfy the rapid growth in fans seeking sports information on the World Wide Web. A Media Numbers Associates study commissioned by Baseball Nut found that 55% of American Web users visited a sports-related Web site in the last 12 months.

"We project the amount of sports-related World Wide Web visitors to triple in the next six months," said Irv Drasnin. "Baseball Nut will provide an attractive fact-filled electronic venue for these passionate fans, a venue that's open 24 hours a day."

####

for additional information contact:

Babe Robinson
(800) 555-BALL
Email: babe@baseballnut.com
Web Site: http://www.baseballnut.com

2

How Search Engines Think

"Matchmaker, matchmaker, make me a match." These lyrics from *Fiddler on the Roof* seem to sum up much of the sentiment attached to wanting to attract visitors to a Web site. As a Web site promoter, you know that perfect visitors exist—but how do you connect with them? How do you get them to find you? Luckily, Web matchmakers exist; in fact, they are so important that the whole Web depends on them. These Web matchmakers look over what different sites have to offer, write it all down, and, when someone queries for that perfect site, supply the seeker with a list of likely URLs. As you've already guessed, these matchmakers are the search engines.

Unfortunately, the Web is a bit more complicated than the village of Anatevka in Czarist Russia, the town in *Fiddler on the Roof.* To begin with, the on-line global village hosts a variety of matchmakers that seem similar; but if you ask each one for that same perfect site, you will most likely receive a variety of answers. To make matters worse, the matchmakers of the global village subtly change how they operate, usually without telling anyone. On top of that, these matchmakers tend to be secretive and spend much of their time striving for dominance over the others in the business.

Search engines may represent the single most important way that people come to your site, but many web site promoters believe that how their site shows up in a search is completely beyond their control. Nothing could be further from the truth. There are ways to make your site more attractive to the search engines. This doesn't mean that you fool search engines (although that's sometimes done), rather, it means that you influence them to increase the chances that people who want to find your site will do so.

This chapter introduces the concepts behind search engines (those spider indexers, general directories, and hermaphrodites I introduced in Chapter 1). It looks at the three-step process of a search: how the search engines examine you, what they remember about you in their databases, and how they rank you in a search result. This information may be a review for those who have already delved into the vagaries and mysteries of search engines. If you nod sagely when I say "meta tag," you may want to skip this chapter and move on to the next, *Making Search Engines Do Your Bidding*, which discusses how you can clarify and focus your identity with the search engines. For the rest of you, read on to get a good primer on matchmaking in the global village.

How They Examine You

So you want to have the "perfect match" find you? Oh, you want to have the perfect 100,000 matches find you? Not to worry, let the search engine help you. Being found via a query to a search engine is a simple way to generate a great number of matches; "being found" is, however, only the final result of a multi-step process. In the first step, you make your site known to the search engine. The search engine will then check it out, and then periodically, it will return to see if it has changed.

First Contact

Usually you'll want to notify different search engines of your existence, but sometimes a search engine will find you and include you in its database without you having to do a thing.

From Web

The average site with links to other sites will be found by most search engines sooner or later. Even directories like Yahoo that rely principally on submissions use spiders as a supplemental means of adding URLs. As the Yahoo FAQ (Frequently Asked Questions) states: "The second way Yahoo! get its links is through automated search robots that look for new announcements at various places." Similarly, sites included in Excite's NetDirectory "are added manually by professional journalists who search the Web for pages to review. They also take a look at some of the pages entered with our 'Suggest Site' button at the bottom of our search page."

From Submissions

As described above, you may be found in spite of your shy nature, but why wait? Submitting your URL to a search engine is easy.

All search engines take submissions directly from the Web. Just go to a search engine site and look for a link or a button that's labeled something like, "Add URL." For example, if you click the Add URL button on Alta Vista's search screen, you move to their Submitting New URLs section (see Figure 2-1). There you type in the URL of your site and, if all works as advertised, Alta Vista takes care of the rest, sending out its spider, Scooter, to delve into the contents of your site.

Alta Vista, like most major search engines, also receives URL submissions from services that automatically submit to multiple sites. To use a submissions service you fill out a form and the service does the rest, submitting your URL to a variety of search engines. I discuss submission services in Chapter 3, *Making Search Engines Do Your Bidding.*

Search Depth

Once the search engine knows about you, it sends out a spider or a human to check you out. These examinations vary in their depth. Some search engines just look at your top page, which is known as a first level search. Others perform a second level search, examining all pages on your site linked to the top page. Some go still deeper. Only one search engine, HotBot, claims to dig all the way down, unearthing and indexing all the pages within a site.

Submitting New URLs

- Please submit only one URL. Our spider will explore your site by following links.
- Do not submit a description or keywords with a URL. To control the abstract served back with your page, check the Help section for the use of the META tag.
- Remember that URLs are case-sensitive, and please check your spelling.

http://

Submit URL

Figure 2–1 Alta Vista's Submitting New URLs section.

Update Frequency

After a search engine has examined you, it will return periodically to see if you've spruced yourself up. The length of time it takes a search engine to completely refresh its entire database varies considerably between search engines (and is a matter of some debate among the different search engine companies). Search engines push to increase their refresh rate, because this quality is perceived by the public as an indication of high quality. Not surprisingly, search engines that rely on spiders are the fastest in rechecking everything in their databases. Some of them, such as Excite, claim to refresh their entire database in a week. Others, such as WebCrawler, seem to take over a month.

How They Remember You

When the search engine examines your site, it notes down various things about you in its database of information. It is this database that is searched when someone makes a query of the search engine.

In the Web's infancy the few existing search engines had databases that consisted of an "inverted index"—essentially a giant grid. Each row in the grid represented a unique URL, and each column represented a unique word. The grid was enormous, because it had to hold all the existing URLs along the left column, and every different word contained in all the URLs along the top row. If a word existed in a particular URL, that intersection of the grid held a check. So if your site dealt with hot dogs, then your row would probably have checks under words like "mustard," "boil," and "bun."

Present-day search engine databases are more sophisticated versions of this simple idea; they record considerably more than the mere presence or absence of a word. Most spider indexes, like Alta Vista, store, in a condensed form, all of the text of your site (except the remarks that are hidden in the HTML code). Other search engines remember a subset of the information from your site, or they derive, deduce, or create information that they deem relevant to your site and remember that.

What search engines remember is critical to how you design a site to be search engine friendly. The information a search engine records becomes the data it uses to plug into its algorithms that determine inquiry rankings. For example, because Alta Vista essentially stores an entire Web site, Alta Vista can search for word proximity. Lycos, however, doesn't keep proximity information, so that search method is unavailable. And because Lycos stores a keyword-heavy digest of a site, its weighting algorithms are skewed toward keyword results.

Here's what search engines remember:

Word Placement and Repetition

Some of the words a search engine finds on a site are considered more important than others; these words will make stronger matches in inquiries. Most search engines see word placement and repetition as indicators of the word's importance. The following is a guide to word placement and repetition.

In the title

Most search engines record the title of the URL and weigh the title's contents heavily in search results. This makes the choice of words in your title extremely important. Even so, having the right keywords in your title does not ensure that you will be found. A search for Cleveland Indians on Alta Vista did not produce the home page for the team within the first 100 results, even though the page is entitled, "Cleveland Indians Baseball Official Site, Home of the Tribe!".

Near the beginning

Most search engines record a word's proximity to the start of the page. These search engines usually consider words located near the beginning of the home page as more important than the same words appearing later in the text. This, coupled with the fact that some search engines use the first block of visible characters on a page as their summary (see "Meta Tags") means that web page designers must be careful selecting what text to include at the beginning of a page.

Repeated

If I were trying to design a search engine and I wanted to have a method of determining which words in documents were more important than others, I'd probably latch onto repetition pretty early. It makes sense that repeated words (aside from common words like *a*, *the*, *but*, and so on) can be viewed as important words.

Many early search engines used word repetition as a measure of word importance. The more often the word was included on a site, the more important it became in determining that site's being matched with that word during a search. However, it didn't take long for Web site designers to realize that by *word packing*—repeating the same word over and over again—they could artificially skew search results. Some search sites countered this manipulation by filtering out often repeated words. The word packers then developed methods of repeating words to squeeze through the filters. After much back and forth, the search engines have pretty much landed in two camps in their response to word packing. Some, like Alta Vista, don't bother checking for it. Others, like Lycos, will place sites farther down in a list if word packing is suspected. Unfortunately, this "packing penalty" also affects sites that may legitimately use a word a number of times.

Meta Tags

Perhaps the most underutilized and misunderstood element in site design is the meta tag. *Meta tags* comprise information placed in the Head element of an HTML document. This meta information won't be displayed by Web browsers but can be accessed by spiders and other types of information retrievers visiting your site. Meta tags provide Web designers with some badly needed control over the keywords and site description that a search engine uses. Unfortunately, not all search engines recognize meta tags, and many search engines are not very forthcoming about whether they do or not. The Web Developer's Virtual Library *Meta Tagging for Search Engines* `http://www.stars.com/Search/Meta/Tag.html` does a good job of keeping abreast of meta tag developments that relate to search engines.

Although an entire class of meta tags exists for HTML, only two need to be considered when dealing with search engines: description and keywords. A description meta tag supplies search engines with a brief paragraph that is displayed as the abstract, or summary, of your site in a search result. Most search engines that don't recognize meta tags just use the first visible portion of text in your document as the summary in their search results.

Here's an example of how the simple insertion of a description meta tag can change how a site appears in a search engine listing. Figure 2-2 shows the appearance of Baseball Bob's Statistical Mecca in an Alta Vista search result.

Baseball Bob's Statistical Mecca
1995 Season. 1994 Season. 1993 Season. 1992 Season. 1991 Season.
1990 Season. 1989 Season. 1988 Season. 1987 Season. 1986.
http://www.baseballbob.com/stats/ - size 16K - 30 Dec 96

Figure 2–2 Baseball Bob result before using a description meta tag.

By including the following text in the Head section of the HTML, the summary that Alta Vista displays will be changed to something much more appealing and understandable (see Figure 2-3).

```
<meta name="description" content="Baseball Stats! Baseball
Links! Baseball Crazy! Come visit the Sultan of Stats at the
Web's fastest growing baseball site.">
```

Baseball Bob's Statistical Mecca
Baseball Stats! Baseball Links! Baseball Crazy! Come visit the Sultan of Stats at the Web's fastest growing baseball site.
http://www.baseballbob.com/stats/ - size 15K - 30 Dec 96

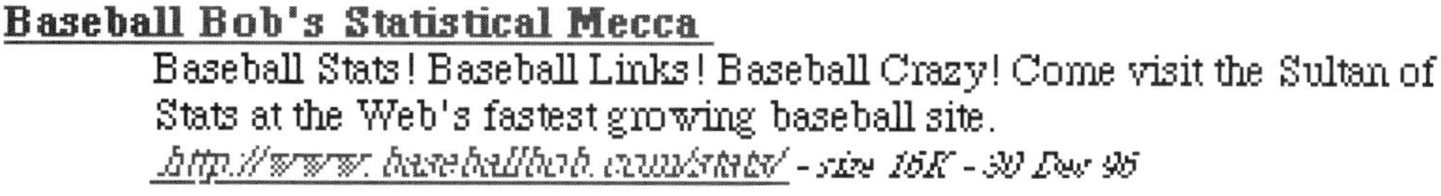

Figure 2–3 Baseball Bob with a description meta tag.

In a similar manner, the keywords meta tag enables the site designer to influence search results by providing the search engine additional keywords to use in its search algorithms. Baseball Bob might include the following text in the Head section of the HTML document.

```
<meta name="keywords" content="baseball statistics, RBI,
runs batted in, HR, home runs, K, strikeouts, ERA, earned
run average">
```

Links

A number of search engines, such as Lycos and Magellan, record how many other sites link to your page as a way of measuring your site's popularity. These search engines then use site popularity as a determining factor in positioning a site in a search result: the more popular a site is, the higher it is ranked by the search engine.

Categories

Finally, some search engines, most notably the general directories, remember you by a subject category. Yahoo's analysts place you in the hierarchical subject category that they think is appropriate, although they will ask you to identify what category you want to be in. Excite, however, uses its artificial intelligence routines to place you in a machine-based category.

How They Rank You

After the search engine checks out your site and records its impressions, the collected data sits, waiting for the query that will produce your Web site at the top of the search results. In practice, search engines rarely produce what someone really wants as the top item in the first screen of results. And, indeed, that may be too much to ask. Some search engine companies profess satisfaction when they produce a good match within the first 30 results.

Everyone wants to know how search engines rank pages, that is, what algorithms they use to produce their results. All search engine companies, either rightly or wrongly, keep most of this information secret presumably to gain a competitive advantage over the other search engines and to prevent site designers from tricking the engines. Many engines, like Open Text, provide essentially no useful information on how they rank searches. A few engines, like HotBot, provide a good deal of information on their weighting methodology. To get a feel for what information is available, check out what HotBot, the most open of the search engines, reveals:

"Each document which matches the requirements of a search is assigned a score. HotBot considers a number of factors when computing these scores. Some of the most basic factors affecting query result scoring include:

- Word frequency in a document. In general, the more often a query word occurs in the document, the higher the score. However, the obscurity of the word also has impact. Common words like "the" contribute less to the score than rare and discriminating words like "tiki."
- Search words in title. Pages that use your search terms in the title will be ranked significantly higher than documents that contain the search term in the text only.
- Search words in keywords. Pages that use your search terms in the "keywords" meta tag will be weighted more highly than text words, but less highly than title words.
- Document length. When the search words appear frequently in a short document, the page will be ranked higher than when the words appear in a long document.

HotBot's proprietary ranking technology is derived from a competition-winning scoring algorithm, which over a large corpus of documents has demonstrated the highest perceived relevance to "typical" users. The HotBot engineers are constantly improving this formula."

Although this information is useful to a site designer, it doesn't give much to go on. Most of what is known about how search engines rank results comes from trial and error, and from Web designers and administrators who share their practical experience. Two of the best sources for this information on the Web are *The Webmaster's Guide to Search Engines and Directories* `http://calafia.com/webmasters/` and *Search Engine Tutorial* `http://www.digital-cafe.com/~webmaster/nw01_05.htm`.

I investigate the nitty gritty of search engine ranking in the next chapter, *Making Search Engines Do Your Bidding.*

3

Making Search Engines Do Your Bidding

Once, I had three girlfriends, each in a different town. For a while my juggling act worked well although it required effort and quick thinking. But when I started to receive hints and then demands to get serious I had to make a choice. I couldn't dedicate myself to one girlfriend and keep the others happy.

Such is the case with search engines. Although you may be able to keep some of them extremely interested in your site, it is impossible to optimize your position with all of them. You can satisfy many of them if you don't expect too much in return, but if you want a lot, you have to choose those that are the most important to you.

There is no magic formula to make your site appear in the first ten results from all search engines. If you could manipulate search engines so easily, they would quickly change their ranking algorithms to defeat you. But you can modify your site so that you make a good impression with most search engines, and make yourself particularly attractive to a few. It's not always easy, because, like personal relationships, the relationships between search engines and sites can sometimes be adversarial. Many search engines view any attempt to improve rankings as unethical. However, I don't see anything wrong with sites trying to improve their results fairly, so that people who are searching for the site will find it more quickly and easily.

The advantage of a search engine is that it is always on, plugging away for you, delivering a steady number of referrals to your site. Although search engines may be important, remember that they are only one part of the mix in Web site promotion. Don't become hung up on squeezing the last drop out of the results. After building a solid foundation with the search engines, you will benefit from promoting your site in places where you are more likely to be noticed by your target audience: magazine reviews, links from related sites, or notices in mailing lists and newsgroups. Making the right connection with any of these may result in more referrals than a search engine.

In this chapter, I describe the ways you can accentuate and tweak your site to make it look better to the various search engines. Then I describe nine influential search engines and discuss their peculiarities and how you can best approach each.

Secrets for High Rankings

Methods to influence search engine ranking fall into the general areas of how you submit your site to them, how to modify your site to improve your rankings, and how often you resubmit. Many of the secrets for scoring high on search results are available on the Web. Like most of the Web, search engines change constantly. To stay abreast of what's current in search engines, check out *The Webmaster's Guide to Search Engines and Directories* `http://calafia.com/webmasters/` and *Search Engine Tutorial* `http://www.digital-cafe.com/~webmaster/nw01_05.htm`.

Submission

Besides their relative importance to Web site promotion, I discuss search engines early in this book because you may have to wait after you submit a site to have it listed. Because of this, it's a good idea to begin the submission process soon. Although search engines may claim otherwise, some often take more than six weeks to list you after you submit.

Although many search engine spiders will find you without your lifting a finger, you need to check each search engine to ensure you have been included in its database. If not, you can submit your URL to each search engine individually, or you can use a shotgun approach.

Manual Submission

Most of the major search engines provide you with a method of submitting your URLs to them. Generally, you will see a prominent link to a submission page from their main search form, but just in case you can't find it, I list the specific address of the submission page for each of the search engines listed in "Persuading the Top Search Engines."

When you submit to search engines, keep in mind that search engines vary regarding the depth they will index in your site. When they are known, I provide the levels to which each search engine will index, below. You may need to submit your deeper pages separately to those search engines that make only a shallow search.

Automatic Submission

If you are like many site owners I've spoken to, you don't think you have the time to submit your site to each individual search engine. I believe the results of individual submission are worth the time you invest, but in the meantime, a backup exists in the form of automatic submission services. The advantage to using an automatic submission site (also called an autoposting site) is that you only have to fill out one form, and the submission service takes care of the rest. The downside is that you cannot tailor your submission to each site.

Most Web masters consider Scott Bannister's Submit-It `http://www.submit-it.com` to be the best of the automatic submission services. Scott has two services, one free and one paid. The free service submits your site to 15 search engines, announce sites, and directories, including Alta Vista, Yahoo, and WebCrawler. Scott's pay service submits your site to over 200 locations that he feels represent the best, most relevant places to list. The free service has the smart option of allowing you to decide which of the 15 sites you want to submit to—so if you don't want to automatically submit to Yahoo because you have already sent them some material (and you don't want to appear to be spamming them), you can uncheck the Yahoo box and they will be left off the list.

Another automatic submission site, Add It! `http://www.liquidimaging.com/liqimg/submit/usa/index.html` will send your URL to 30 important sites, including most that I list in my top nine, below. Unfortunately, Add It! doesn't allow you to deselect a site from the list.

If you feel the need to check out other submission services, you can find a long list of them at Yahoo `http://www.yahoo.com/Computers_and_Internet/Internet/World_Wide_Web/Announcement_Services/`. I discuss automatic submission services further in Chapter 4, *How to Get Links from Hundreds of Sites.*

Keywords

I mentioned in Chapter 1, *A Million Ways to Get Hits,* that one of the most important exercises you can go through when you begin to promote your Web site is to define your keywords. Essentially, keywords are those search terms your prospective visitor enters into the "search for" box when trying to find your site. Like many site developers, you may have trouble finding the best keywords because you are suffering from site myopia—the inability to see your own site clearly. The keywords that you think best describe your site may not be those that your potential visitors will use.

Often, the best strategy to develop the most effective keywords is to form a focus group comprised of potential site visitors, friends, and colleagues, and have them generate keywords for your site. Ask them what words they would give a search engine when looking for your site. Then look at the words and see if you can generate any common variations on them, such as by changing tense or number. For example, a site on the greatest baseball sluggers may want to include hit, hitter, and hitters as some of the keywords.

Once you have a solid list of 10 to 30 keywords, have your focus group rank them in importance and descriptiveness. Choose two or three words at the top of the lists as your heavy-hitter keywords. Then be sure to include these keywords in your title, headings, text, and meta tags, as I describe in the rest of this section. Note that some search engines favor unusual words in their search rankings, so some uncommon keywords may be helpful.

Title

The title of a page is displayed in (of all things) the title bar and is programmed in the Head section of your HTML using the <title> tag. Most search engines display the title of the page in search results, and many give added weight to title words in their ranking algorithms. For these reasons, you should make your page titles descriptive and be sure to use your heavy-hitter keywords in your titles. The title of your home page is the most important to consider, but don't forget the other pages on your site. Most search engines include deeper pages, so remember to include your keywords there, also. The titles of deeper pages can include keywords of less importance.

Some search engines and directories list similar results alphabetically, so sometimes you see some rather odd page titles. Titles like "AAAAA Brewing Supplies" and "!!!!Popcorn Express!!!!!" have been conjured by site designers who are desperate to reach the top of an alphabetically sorted list, perhaps disregarding the negative impact that such grasping names may have on their readers. Your site will provide more impact with a well-considered title, in spite of its alphabetic rank.

Meta Tags

I discussed in the last chapter, *How Search Engines Think*, the HTML coding for meta tags. The keyword and description meta tags that you include in your pages provide information to search engines that will not be displayed by Web browsers.

There is seldom any harm in using meta tags, and since they are easy to create, you should try to include them on your pages. If a search engine does not recognize your meta tags as such, the words will be indexed along with the rest of the text in the site. Note: search engines that penalize for word repetition may count your meta tag keywords and put you over their accepted limit.

Description meta tags can be especially helpful to a site that has frame information or JavaScript at the start of its pages. Without meta tags, a search engine may use the first characters on the page as the site's summary in the search results. If this is frame or JavaScript-related information, it will appear to the searcher as gobbledygook instead of as a good description of the site. Figure 3-1 shows a search result of a page using frames.

83% **Baseball Nut** [More Like This]
URL: http://www.baseball_crazy/out/of/control/
Summary: The Baseball Nut Web-pages requires a browser with FRAMES support, such as Netscape 2.0. -- Others browsers can't see the same pages without the FRAMES interface yet, but will as soon as I get the time.

Figure 3–1 Frame information used as a summary.

A more pleasing result can be obtained using the description meta tag, as in Figure 3-2.

83% **Baseball Nut** [More Like This]
URL: http://www.baseball_crazy/out/of/control/
Summary: The Baseball Nut has got to be cracked! Check us out for scores, standings, trivia, and a chance to win a trip for two to the World Series!

Figure 3–2 A description meta tag used as a summary.

Text and Page Design

You need to include text on your page so the search engine spiders can read and index it. Be very careful when you design your Web page that you don't include too much of your text in graphics. First, graphics are slow to load, and this alone may exhaust your visitors' patience. Second, text embedded in graphics cannot be read by search engine spiders, so these words will be ignored.

Most search engine spiders will index the alt tags that can be included in the HTML to display when an image is not loaded.

Another consideration in page design is the search engine that doesn't use meta tags as the summary of your site. Often these search engines will use the first 250 or so characters of your site for the summary, although some search engines, like Excite and WebCrawler, choose other text (see "Persuading the Top Search Engines").

Repeated Words

Because repeated words are penalized by some search engines (like Lycos) while used in the ranking algorithms of others (like Alta Vista), page designers are caught in a dilemma. Which search engine friend do you try to appeal to? There is apparently no way to make both happy—hiding "popcorn, popcorn, popcorn, popcorn..." at the bottom of your page may result in high rankings from one search engine in a search for the keyword "popcorn" and low rankings from another.

Although you might not see how you can appease both search engines, never underestimate the resources of a Web site promoter. There is a way around the multiple-word penalty that can be used by someone who is in a legitimate quandary when trying to appear equal to all search engines.

Here's the trick: create repeated-word pages on your site that bounce the visitor directly to a content page. This "bounce script" can be written in a number of different ways, with varying degrees of success with different browsers. The simplest script uses a refresh meta tag in the Head section of the HTML. For example, the following code quickly bounces the visitor from the current page to the page "fielder.index.html."

```
<head>
<meta http-equiv="Refresh" content="0;
URL=fielder.index.html">
<title>One Moment, Please</title>
</head>
```

You could, of course, use any title for the page. The 0 after the `content=` represents the number of seconds before the bounce, so if (for some reason) you wanted the page to stick around for two seconds before the bounce you would use the following code.

```
<meta http-equiv="Refresh" content="2;
URL=fielder.index.html">
```

This trick works for most modern browsers. Please understand that I am not advocating the use of this procedure to abuse either your visitor or the search engines. But until the search engines can conform to something approaching a standard of assessing word repetition, even an ethical site promoter must sometimes resort to smoke and mirrors to produce a fair result.

Links

Both *internal links* (the links between the pages on your site) and *external links* (the links between other sites and yours) can influence the behavior of search engines.

Into site

Some search engines examine only the top page of your site; others follow links from that first page and look one step deeper into your site, and others will go deeper still. When the information is known, I've listed how deep each search engine digs in "Persuading the Top Ten Tools."

Multilevel digging poses a problem, but you can use two strategies to help search engines index the relevant material on your site. First, place your substantive pages in the top levels of your site, and link to them generously. Having done this, even the medium digging search engines should then find your most important material with the submission of your home page URL. Second, lead the shallow digging search engines deeper by submitting to them the URLs of your more important pages at deeper strata within your site. This procedure may take more time, but can increase traffic dramatically as people arrive at all levels of your site, not just the top.

From other sites

Some search engines reason that a site's popularity relates to its quality, and therefore a popular site should show up higher in a search result than a less popular one. But since a search engine can't determine the real number of visitors to any site, how can popularity be ascertained? Search engines can record what sites link to others on the Web, and they use the reasoning that the more links to a site, the more popular the site is. One can argue with this. After all, the number of links to a site may only be an indication of the fervor with which a site has sought links, or a measure of a site's general nature, or an indication of how long-lived the site is, rather than an indication of high quality. Nevertheless, since a search engine can quantify the numbers of links to a site, this figure may be used in determining search results.

Although links to your site may influence ranking by some search engines, they are even more important as triggers for site visits. As a result, links to your site should be vigorously sought as part of a successful promotion campaign. I discuss links to your site in Chapter 4, *How to Get Quality Links*, Chapter 5, *How to Get Links from Hundreds of Sites*, and Chapter 9, *Launching Your Web Ad Campaign*.

Updates

The rule here is: resubmit everything if your URL changes. Make sure that as you develop your site you submit the new, deeper URLs to the shallow digging search engines. Likewise, when you edit your site, make sure the edits are reflected in your description and keyword meta tags.

In order to appear fresh to the search engines, those who are ethically challenged will periodically change their page titles and creation dates. Some search engines will interpret a page with a new title or creation date as an entirely new page and list it in the search results in one place, with the old page (still with the correct link) listed in another place. Page titles, of course, can be easily changed in the HTML. Creation dates generally need to be modified by your server's administrator, although in some situations you may be able to modify the creation date by replacing the file on the server.

Persuading the Top Search Engines

In this section, I discuss ten important search engines and how you can work with their strengths and weaknesses. But the search engines, by their varied natures, make it difficult for you to treat them equally. How do you decide which search engines should be the stuff dreams are made of? Any site promoter must seriously consider Yahoo, Alta Vista, WebCrawler, and Excite as influential and worth courting. The new kid, InfoSeek Ultra, will probably move up in the charts. And what about the rest?

I have the temerity to list these top ten search engines in what I consider to be a *rough* order of importance to the site promoter. But I do so with these caveats. First, I am providing only a *current* snapshot of the search engines, knowing that the Web is mutable and that, over time, some of these stars will fade and others will burst into prominence. Second, I am sure some experts will argue with my ranking for legitimate reasons (and I shudder when I imagine what some of the search engine marketers might say). Finally, and most importantly, since search engines vary in their value to different sites, you will need to determine over time which engines work best for you. However, the bottom line is that all of these search engines can generate hits, so I would not want to pass on any of them.

Yahoo

Yahoo http://www.yahoo.com, originated as a small project of two graduate students at Stanford University and has grown into the most influential general directory on the Web. Not only is Yahoo popular but its listings are under human control, which means you may be able to affect how your site is listed.

Submission

Although Yahoo will pick up some listings from Web announce sites, the vast majority of its content comes from manual submissions. If you click on the Add URL link at the top of any Yahoo page, you will move to the page for making submissions http://add.yahoo.com/bin/add?. However, Yahoo suggests that the best way to submit is first to check to see if your site is already listed. If not, go to the Yahoo category in which you think you should be listed and click the Add URL on that page; the category field for the Add URL will be automatically filled in for you. Yahoo's submission help area http://www.yahoo.com/docs/info/addfaq.html#detail should answer any questions you have about the process. Keep in mind that what you submit in the comments field will be displayed as the summary of your site by Yahoo, so make sure it is descriptive and compelling. And if you think that your site should be listed in more than one Yahoo category, include that information in the additional categories field.

After you make a submission and Yahoo's editors decide your site should be included, you will receive e-mail stating that your site will appear within 24-48 hours. Sometimes it takes a bit longer; after all, these are people you're dealing with. If you need to change a listing, use the Yahoo form for that procedure: http://add.yahoo.com/bin/change.

Yahoo's editors use their discretion when considering how deeply they investigate your site. If you have deep pages that you think should be included in Yahoo, submit them separately (see *Notes*, below). Yahoo will keep sites listed as long as they are functional. However, your site may be moved to a different category without notice.

Notes

Yahoo doesn't support meta tags. Instead, Yahoo's editors use the comments that you submitted as your site's summary to determine the keywords to be used. You can have some influence on the keyword selection by including likely candidates in the title and comments field when you submit. Page popularity is apparently not used in determining whether a site will be listed with Yahoo.

Lucy Mohl, developer of the vast film and video site Film.com, says, "Most people think of the Web as an impersonal place, I see it as a place filled with people." She puts that perspective into practice in her relationship with the Yahoo editor that handles the category in which her site is listed. Lucy tries to take advantage of the service Yahoo offers while making sure she does not abuse the relationship, and she feels that has worked to her advantage. Film.com is unusual in that it has hundreds of film review pages listed under different Yahoo categories. Even so, Yahoo will automatically reject batch submissions from Film.com or any site if too many URLs are submitted at once. The key to dealing with Yahoo is to remember that you are building a relationship with an editor, even though it may be through e-mail and submissions forms.

Although Yahoo may say otherwise, having a good relationship with your Yahoo editor probably helps your site being included in Yahoo's What's Cool category. Sites that Yahoo considers cool carry a little sunglasses icon—presumably quite helpful in increasing hits.

Alta Vista

Alta Vista `http://www.altavista.digital.com`, the first of the big and fast searchers, caused a sensation when it suddenly appeared on the Web in December 1995. Designed and maintained by the Digital Equipment Corporation, Alta Vista is based on a 64-bit Digital Alpha server running at 266MHz and offers one of the largest databases of any search engine. Alta Vista is so large that searches often produce overwhelming numbers of results and may be difficult to wade through. For best results, searchers should usually use Alta Vista's advanced search features, but you can't expect your potential visitors to do so.

Submission

Alta Vista's spider will likely pick up your site if any links to it exist on the Web. If you aren't in the database, you can give Alta Vista a poke by clicking on the Add URL link `http://www.altavista.digital.com/cgi-bin/query?pg=tmpl&v=addurl.html` at the bottom of any Alta Vista page. Alta Vista claims that once you submit, their spider will visit your site and you will be available for a search within a day. However, it often takes much longer than that, sometimes up to six weeks. Alta Vista's spider (Scooter) digs about three levels down in your site, so if you have deep pages you want listed, you will need to submit lower URLs. Scooter then digs three levels down from there, so don't go overboard with submissions.

Like InfoSeek's Ultra, Alta Vista's spider will vary how often it rechecks your site based on its observations of how often your site changes. The entire Alta Vista database is refreshed about once a month.

Notes

Alta Vista supports both keyword and description meta tags. If no description meta tag is included, Alta Vista will use the first 250 or so characters on your page as a summary.

Because of Alta Vista's immense size and the generality of its ranking algorithms, your keywords take on increased importance. Ranking algorithms heavily weight both keywords near the beginning of the page and keywords found near one another. The most likely way for you to show up on the first page of an Alta Vista search result is if the searcher has submitted multiple search words that are all included in your keyword meta tag.

Alta Vista doesn't search for word variants, so you need to include variants of your important keywords in your keyword meta tag. Alta Vista does not penalize repeated words but doesn't increase the rankings of pages with repeated words, either. Page popularity is not used as a ranking consideration.

Excite

Excite `http://www.excite.com`, like Yahoo, originated with Stanford University students. Excite includes a large database and takes a novel approach to search engine design by using "artificial intelligence" to extract a site's dominant theme. This intelligence, named Intelligent Concept Extraction, assumes that words found near each other are conceptually related. Working from these conceptual relationship, Intelligent Concept Extraction generates a site's dominant theme, which becomes the standard against which searcher's queries are measured to match and rank the site. This approach seems to work well much of the time, although it can occasionally produce some bizarre results. You may need to tweak your site if you want to perform well in an Excite search.

Submission

Excite suggests that you check to see if your site is already included in their database. If not, clicking on the Add URL link will take you to Excite's submission page `http://www.excite.com/Search/add_url.html?amt`. If you submit your top URL, Excite will follow links down two more layers. If you want Excite to index deeper material, you must additionally submit deeper URLs. Excite's documentation implies that you will be listed in their database two weeks after submission, but times up to six weeks are more likely.

Notes

Excite doesn't support either keyword or description meta tags. In order to conjure up a description, Excite uses its dominant theme algorithms to select a few of the punctuated sentences on your site. Similarly, keywords are chosen from your text. In order to help Excite do a good job, you should include concise, descriptive sentences near the top of your pages. Avoid using misleading material such as jokes and quotations. You will also perform better in searches if some of your descriptive words are uncommon.

If you don't like being at the mercy of artificial intelligence, it is possible to persuade Excite to use your own description for its summary in a search result. The trick is to imbed multiple copies of the description in a comments line in the HTML. (Comments in HTML exist for the programmer to make notes and will not be displayed by a browser.) For example, the following HTML would probably convince Excite to use your description.

```
<!--
We worship hot dogs. Come see the largest variety of mail
order wieners on the Web.
We worship hot dogs. Come see the largest variety of mail
order wieners on the Web.
We worship hot dogs. Come see the largest variety of mail
order wieners on the Web.
-->
```

Excite uses page popularity as a factor in search results, although it doesn't seem to be weighted heavily. Excite claims it rebuilds its database once a week—a claim that seems genuine.

In the past, sites have disappeared from Excite's database for no apparent reason. Be sure to monitor Excite periodically to make sure you are still included. If you disappear, just resubmit your site.

InfoSeek Ultra

InfoSeek Ultra `http://ultra.infoseek.com/` represents the next generation in spider indexes. InfoSeek Ultra features fast submission times, a large section of the Web indexed, quick search times, and searches that can include even common words (like *a, an, the*). Perhaps more importantly, InfoSeek Ultra provides a significant amount of information for the Web site promoter on how to be ranked fairly. By providing such information, search engines like InfoSeek Ultra and HotBot attempt to level the playing field, for which they should receive our thanks. Such openness reflects a confidence that these search engines' ranking algorithms are safe from unfair tampering.

Submission

Here's the future. Click on InfoSeek Ultra's Add URL link `http://ultra.infoseek.com/AddUrl?pg=addurl.html&sv=US&lk=1`, fill in your URL, and click the update button. Your site will be available on the search engine within minutes. Try it!

When I analyzed InfoSeek Ultra, the spider would not dig into any linked pages on a site. In order to get more pages included, you could submit each page individually or send e-mail (ultra-addurl-request@infoseek.com) with one page listed per line. Ultra may have changed this procedure by now, so be sure to check the submission page.

Ultra incorporates the unusual feature of monitoring how often your site changes and modifying how often its spider visits your site based on that information. For example, if you add or change pages every couple of days, Ultra will visit your site more often than if your site changes only every couple of months.

Notes

Ultra supports both keyword and description meta tags. If meta tags don't exist, Ultra falls back on the usual procedure of indexing all the text on the page (except comments) and uses the first characters on the page as the summary displayed in the search result.

Ultra is the one search engine that claims to find all word variants during a search. For the Web designer, this means that you don't have to include variations on your major keywords as you do with most other search engines. For example, a search for the word "mouse" will also search for "mice."

Ultra incorporates a repeat filter that prevents repeated words from affecting rankings. Ultra's ranking algorithms stress keywords and phrases in the title and the beginning of the document. Higher scores will be obtained by a document containing more of the query terms; in addition, uncommon words are given more weight.

HotBot

HotBot `http://www.hotbot.com`, HotWired's search engine, features a parallel processing scheme developed for the Inktomi search engine at Berkeley. HotBot's strengths include the large amount of the Web indexed, the depth to which it catalogs a site, and fast search times and database refreshing. For the Web designer, perhaps the most worthwhile aspect of HotBot is its willingness to provide some information on ranking algorithms. HotBot also supports a mechanism in which you can report low scoring.

Submission

HotBot's spider rebuilds its database about once a week and will include sites that have links from other sites. However, if you discover that HotBot has not found you, you can submit your site directly to HotBot using the Add URL link `http://www.hotbot.com/full/addurl.html`. You only need to add your top page, and HotBot will index your entire site.

Notes

HotBot supports keyword and description meta tags, so be sure to include them in your pages. HotBot's ranking algorithms stress keywords in the title, then keywords in meta tags, then frequency of keywords in text. Uncommon words are given more weight. Apparently, HotBot does not use page popularity as a ranking scheme, but there has been some suggestion that it might in the future.

HotBot claims it will improve the search algorithms based on customer feedback. To that end, HotBot asks you to report "what you consider to be obviously silly rankings" to `feedback@hotbot.com`.

WebCrawler

WebCrawler `http://www.webcrawler.com`, a moderately powerful search engine with a relatively small database, was originally developed at the University of Washington. WebCrawler used to have a disproportionate influence on the Web because it was owned by America Online and was the default search engine for AOL members. Since WebCrawler's sale to Excite in late 1996, its future importance is unclear.

WebCrawler only stores "popular" pages in its database, which it determines by counting the number of external links to a page. WebCrawler provides a mechanism to check how many links it has recorded to you; just go to `http://www.webcrawler.com/WebCrawler/Links.html`, fill in your URL, and you will see who WebCrawler knows is pointing to you.

Submission

WebCrawler relies on a spider (Spidey) to gather sites, so you should check to see if you are already in the database. WebCrawler makes this easy for you; just go to `http://www.webcrawler.com/WebCrawler/Status.html`. By filling in your URL, WebCrawler will tell you if Spidey has visited your site (and when).

If Spidey doesn't know you exist, submit your site by clicking on the Add URL link `http://www.webcrawler.com/WebCrawler/SubmitURLS.html`. Fill in the URL for your top page and any other pages you want WebCrawler to consider for inclusion (Spidey won't dig into your site without encouragement). Now sit back and wait to see if WebCrawler deems you sufficiently popular to be in their database. If so, WebCrawler states that you should appear within two weeks although times as long as six weeks have been reported. The database reportedly refreshes every month, although a few tests on the Status page show this to be an optimistic figure.

Notes

WebCrawler uses a combination of search filters that can be dangerous to a web designer's livelihood. On one hand, WebCrawler says it determines a search ranking by taking the number of times a keyword exists on a page and dividing it by the total number of words on the page. At the same time, WebCrawler believes strongly in punishing those who try to fool it by repeating keywords too often; offending pages are dropped from the database. Exactly how many repetitions trigger this action is unknown. If some of your pages don't appear in an appropriate WebCrawler search, you may need to consider reducing word repetition on them.

WebCrawler uses an unusual search result display scheme. Initially, search results display only the title of a page. By clicking on the Show Summaries button, summaries will also be displayed. But what summaries! WebCrawler uses text from somewhere near the beginning of the document, but it's hard to predict what that text will be. It could include tag text (such as the alt tags used for images). Surprisingly, even though WebCrawler doesn't use meta tag description per se, your meta tag description could end up as the summary by accident. What a way to run a search engine.

Lycos

Lycos `http://www.lycos.com`, developed at Carnegie-Mellon University, is one of the oldest and most eccentric search engines. Unlike most of the spider indexes, Lycos does not index the full text of a page. Instead, it creates an abstract which incorporates titles, headers, and repeated words and phrases. Lycos also runs a directory.

Submission

If other sites link to yours, the Lycos spider will probably find you; however, you can also submit directly at the appropriate page: `http://www.lycos.com/addasite.html`. This submission form supports a feature where you can delete pages from the database. Lycos claims that all the pages in your site will be indexed, but experience shows that the spider only goes about three levels deep, so deeper pages should be submitted separately. Lycos also claims that you will show up two to four weeks after submission, and that claim seems true.

Notes

Lycos supports meta tags, which you should use—if left to its own devices, Lycos doesn't handle the summary well. Without a description meta tag, Lycos creates its own summary which may vary in length and quality. Lycos admits that opening graphics confuse its summary writing.

Lycos's ranking is based on keywords used in the title, in high level headings, and near the beginning of the page. Keywords that are near each other will also increase a ranking. Lycos does have a repetition penalty, but how many words will trigger it is unknown. Lycos uses page popularity in ranking.

Lycos constructs its database cumulatively. If your site remains inactive for about four weeks, you will be dropped. Lycos requests that you delete and resubmit sites that have substantially changed.

Magellan

Magellan `http://www.mckinely.com` is a search engine that is closely tied to a directory that includes reviews. Since Magellan's interface is integrated, (that is, the search engine and the directory are combined), you can receive reviewed and unreviewed material in a search. Magellan was recently bought by Excite, so changes may be in store.

Submission

Magellan provides an Add Site link `http://www.mckinley.com/feature.cgi?add_bd`, but this feature will submit your site for consideration only to the directory, not to the general Web search engine. For that, you must rely on Magellan's spider finding you.

Notes

Magellan spells out their ranking criteria fairly plainly. Top results are given to those pages that include the greatest number of the keywords being searched for. Ranking next depends on whether there are keywords in the title, in the Magellan review, and in the URL. Finally, Magellan gives higher ranking to pages that use the keywords more often. Magellan does not support meta tags.

Open Text Index

Open Text develops and markets text indexing software. Their Open Text Index `http://index.opentext.net/` is maintained "as a live demonstration of the power of our software, which you can purchase or license for your organization."

Open Text Index is an oddball in many ways, offering a strong set of search tools while maintaining a relatively small database of the Web. One may argue that Open Text's biggest fault is how little information it supplies on how their search engine works and how to obtain fair rankings. However, you can *buy* results: Open Text is unique in that you can pay for a guaranteed appearance in the first ten search results for a particular keyword.

Submission

Open Text employs a spider, so you should check to see if the index already includes you. If not, click on the Submit URL link `http://index.opentext.net/main/submitURL.html`. Since Open Text's spider doesn't follow internal links, you will have to submit individually each page you want in their database. It usually takes about eight weeks after submission for a site to appear. Catalog refresh reportedly occurs monthly, although some have experienced considerably longer periods. You should resubmit your site if you have modified it significantly.

Notes

Open Text Index's procedure of determining the summary to use for the search result leaves a lot to be desired. Since it doesn't support meta tags, it won't use a description you supply. Instead, it just takes the first text it finds on the document, including tagged text, and plugs it into the summary. Open Text Index cannot resolve different word endings, so include them in your document.

4

How to Get Quality Links

You've probably invested a great deal of time and resources developing and maintaining your Web presence—whether that means overseeing a crack team of designers, writers, and HTML jockeys or spending long hours in front of a monitor creating graphics and writing the code yourself. As many Web site administrators discover, even small sites seem to take longer to develop than expected (and worse, cost more than what's budgeted), which is why it's important to utilize your time wisely when promoting your Web presence.

One of the best methods of Web site promotion involves getting your site linked from other sites and directories across the Web. Registering your URL with the major search engines is a good start (see Chapter 3, *Making Search Engines Do Your Bidding*), but there's a lot more out there than just search engines. To really capitalize on the hyperlinked nature of the Web, it's important that your potential visitors be able to find you from just about anywhere.

Does this mean you have to persuade every other site on the Web to include a link to your site? Not necessarily. Although there are benefits to having links strewn to every corner of the Internet (see Chapter 5, *How to Get Links from Hundreds of Sites*), the prevailing philosophy among most Web promoters is that a moderate number of high-quality links—links that provide a high number of visitors—is better than thousands of dusty, seldom-used connections.

In this chapter, I'll show you how to determine which sites fall into your high-quality category, where to locate them, and the best ways to contact them to establish a link. Then, as with all discussions of quality, I'll focus on what's the *best*, by detailing the top 10 award lists and how to get your site listed. Lastly, I'll cover the growing field of Web media, and help you navigate through the

PointCast and Reuters news feeds to find out which electronic magazines and news services will give your site a high volume of hits.

Exploring Your Neighborhood

In the film *Throw Momma From the Train*, there's a scene where the middle-aged members of Billy Crystal's writing class read their works aloud. One woman dramatically recites her story of a submarine conflict: "'Dive!' said the Captain into the thing, and the First Mate pushed the button that made the ship dive." For several minutes she goes on like this, inserting nonspecific "things" and "whatsits" to compensate for her lack of submariner knowledge. She failed to follow the maxim given to all beginning writers, "Write what you know."

As you're trolling the Web for sites to link to, it's best to begin in areas with which you're already familiar. Sites that share similar subject matter or interests with your site should be your first stop, because your target audience is already there and waiting to hear about you.

Sites Like Yours

You're no doubt aware of sites that share the same topics or themes as yours. Bookmark these in your browser if you haven't already. To find others, here are a couple of routes you can follow.

The Longer Journey

Drill down through a hierarchical directory like Yahoo, finding entries and topics on sites that are similar to yours. (If nothing is similar to yours, congratulations! Chances are, it won't be like that for long.) This could take some time, but it promises to be rewarding.

The Shorter Journey

Go to a search engine that ranks its findings based on the percentage of matches, such as Excite `http://www.excite.com`. Type four or five of the keywords you came up with in Chapter 1 into the search field, then click the search button. If you've previously submitted your site to search engines (as explained in "Persuading the Top Search Engines" in Chapter 3, *Making Search Engines Do Your Bidding*), locate your listing from the search results, then take a look at who's sharing the neighborhood.

Depending on the search engine, you may also have the option of clicking on "More Like This" (in Excite) or "Similar Pages" (in WebCrawler), which should give you a better idea of which sites are akin to yours (see Figure 4-1).

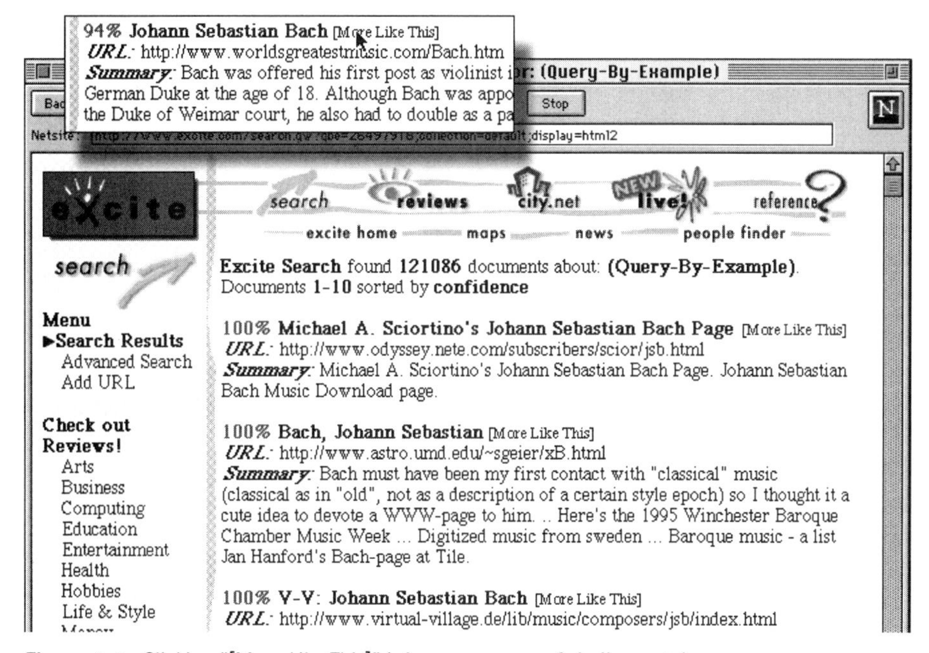

Figure 4–1 Clicking "[More Like This]" brings up a page of similar matches.

Role Reversal

Don't worry, I'm not turning this into a psychological exercise ("Tell me about your home page life...."). Rather, role reversal is a great method of opening up the hidden passages to your Web site.

As any experienced marketer will tell you, knowing your target audience is crucial to success (see sidebar). Put yourself in your visitor's shoes, and think of as many different routes to get to your site as possible. Sometimes it helps to have a friend or a colleague help to provide another viewpoint. You want to approach your site not only from the main entrance, but from all sides; look for side doors, floor hatches, ceiling panels, even virtual ventilation systems.

For example, envision a chain of links leading backwards from your site. What might lead people to your page in three or four links? If you run a site called French Horns Forever, visitors could arrive via topics such as music, instruments, the Renaissance, French history, even croissants and desserts! You want

DIGITAL DEMOGRAPHICS

It's common in a marketing campaign to have a detailed "sketch" of the ideal audience for a product: age, gender, occupation, income level, geographic location, family dynamic (single? married? children?), and a host of other information that paints an accurate picture of the consumer. As the Web matures, more demographic information is becoming available online. A few sites worth checking out are *American Demographics* magazine **http://www.marketingtools.com**, Internet Trends **http://www.genmagic.com/Internet/Trends**, and the Graphics, Visualization, and Usability (GVU) WWW User Survey **http://www-survey.cc.gatech.edu**.

to provide your target audience links to find you from any of these places.

Special Topic Directories and Links Pages

I'm continually surprised at the number of people I run into who know all about the major search engines, but haven't discovered the many specialized engines and links pages that exist for almost any subject you can imagine. Rather than blindly shooting keywords into a large-scale search engine—which usually produces thousands of matches that may have nothing to do with what you're looking for—many people are turning to sites that offer specific topic information.

For example, the WebScout Index Page **http://www.webcom.com/webscout/Search/Engines.html** provides a list of sites such as 80s Search (an engine that looks for information related to the 1980s), Freedom.co.uk (gay, lesbian, bisexual, and transgender Web sites), and Electric Manufacturers on the Web (links to hardware companies). Listing your site in one of these types of indexes will help ensure that your URL isn't lost among a screen full of archived Usenet posts and sites that may contain one of your keywords somewhere.

Realizing that visitors are getting tired of asking for one thing and getting a horde of unrelated information, some of the major engines have also started offering directories with narrower focuses. Yahoo is in the process of launching geographically-concentrated areas such as Yahoo! Japan and **http://www.yahoo.com/docs/info/bridge.html** Yahoo! New York **http://ny.yahoo.com**. Another section, Yahooligans! for Kids **http://www.yahooligans.com**, is aimed specifically at younger visitors.

To find specific engines and directories related to your site's topics, I'd first recommend checking either WebScout's page or Beaucoup! **http://www.beaucoup.com/engines.html**, another great resource with over 600 lists and engines. Then, try some of the major search engines by searching for "[your topic] links." You wouldn't believe how many subject specific links sites exist. In my testing, Excite and HotBot provided the highest-quality lists of links; Alta Vista, on the other hand, produced a large pool of results but suffered from site repetition.

Getting Linked

Unlike search engines, where all you have to do is submit your URL and basic information, getting linked to other Web sites requires persistence, personality, and an occasional prodding. After all, you're most likely dealing with people who are as hardworking and stressed-out as you are, not a robotic spider or auto-reply feature.

Contacting Other Sites

The simplest method to contact sites is through e-mail. Unless it's absolutely critical that a link to your site be created *immediately*, don't bother telephoning (if, that is, the site even includes a phone number). My experience with Webmasters and system administrators suggests that e-mail is the preferred lifeblood of communication for these folk, who are usually updating site content, putting out network fires, or otherwise doing something productive that could be dashed by the intrusion of a phone call. e-mail is easy and—most important—handy to store and read later.

Most Web sites will include an e-mail address somewhere in their site. If you don't find anything on the first or second pages, check to see if there's an About, Contact Information, or Help link.

Every once in a while I run across a Web site that has no e-mail link on it anywhere. Bad Web designer! Bad! If this happens, the first thing to try is the InterNIC Whois service `http://rs.internic.net/cgi-bin/whois`. If you're not familiar with it, InterNIC is the organization that assigns and tracks domain names, and Whois is a method of querying for information on Internet addresses. In most cases, performing a Whois search on the domain name of the site you're trying to reach yields the correct contact (see Figure 4-2).

An alternative approach is to try sending mail to "info," "webmaster," "admin," or "help," followed by "@domain name." So, for example, if you were at the French Horns Forever site `http://www.french-horns-forever.org`, you could try e-mailing "webmaster@french-horns-forever.org".

Whois Query Results

```
Stourwater Productions (ZAP-DOM)
   1619 Eighth Ave. N
   Seattle, WA 98109-3007

   Domain Name: ZAP.COM

   Administrative Contact, Technical Contact, Zone Contact:
      Fleishman, Glenn  (GF41)  glenn@POPCO.COM
      (206) 467-9449 (FAX) (206) 467-9483

   Record last updated on 02-Feb-95.
   Record created on 09-Sep-94.

   Domain servers in listed order:

   STOUT.POPCO.COM              205.199.66.1
   MAIGRET.POPCO.COM            205.199.66.4
   NS1.IXA.NET                  199.242.16.1
   MORSE.POPCO.COM              205.199.66.7
```

Figure 4–2 InterNIC Whois query.

Tailor Your Subject Line

Webmasters and system administrators tend to occupy their time answering e-mail from people who are having problems with their systems. To help filter your message from the inbox of tech-support issues and catch their attention, make sure the Subject line of your e-mail is short, clear, and explanatory.

Correct:

Link

Incorrect:

Please add me to your Linkz page and in return i'll add you 2!!!!

Be Brief

Really, there's no reason to prattle on about the glories of your site, unless you want to decrease your chances of being added. Write a brief comment about your desire to be added as a link to your contact's site, include the 25-word description you wrote in Chapter 1, *A Million Ways to Get Hits,* and remember: include your URL!

Cooperation vs. Competition

One hotly-debated topic among on-line marketers and promoters is the question of whether or not to link to a competitor's Web site. Naturally, there are pros and cons for each approach, and the matter is far from being resolved (if it is even resolvable).

Cooperation: The Web Way

Cooperation, according to its advocates, helps everyone by allowing visitors to share information and make educated choices. Often cooperation takes the form of similar subject sites exchanging links.

From a seller's standpoint, supporters of cooperation argue that sharing information can foster competition. Visitors looking to buy widgets on the Widgets USA site can click over to the Widgets 'R' Us site to compare prices. To remain competitive, each company can raise and lower its prices much the same way stores do in the real world.

Another advantage to cooperation is the increased flexibility afforded to smaller companies that are not able to provide a wealth of information on their site. If Widgets USA is a small startup with limited resources, they may be able to link to information on Widgets 'R' Us that has been provided by the Widget manufacturer without needing to invest the time to collect and present that information on their own. (Before linking to another site's resources, however, be sure to read "Do You Need Permission to Link to Other Sites?", sidebar.)

DO YOU NEED PERMISSION TO LINK TO OTHER SITES?

The use of hyperlinks brings up an issue that no one has previously had to deal with in terms of mass communication. Is it okay just to include a link to someone else's site, or do you need their permission? With other communications vehicles such as magazines, radio, and television, you can probably get away with using a company's phone number or address (depending on the company, of course), but you can't use their media—articles, photos, video clips, sound bites—without permission. The Web, however, allows you to add a link that not only points you in the right direction, but also *takes you there.*

The general Web consensus is that it's acceptable to link to (but not copy files from) other sites without permission, provided that you're not claiming it as a section of your own site. Also, it's best to link to a site's home page, not any of its supporting pages directly. If, for some reason, someone asks you to remove a link, it's good manners to do so.

However, there can be benefits to requesting permission before linking to someone's site. Asking for a link is a good way to initiate ongoing communication with the other site producer, which is useful in the event of URL changes and site modifications. Informing them of your link also helps them track where their traffic is coming from by knowing who is linked to them.

But the greatest reason to exchange links is the potential for bringing more visitors to your site. One site administrator I know has always sought reciprocal links. He has a links page with hundreds of similar links on it, whereas almost all of the pages that link to him have his site as one of the few options on which to click. He is convinced that he receives many times the visitors from links into his site than he loses via links out to other sites. I'll bet he's right.

Competition: No Way

The main downside to linking to a neighbor's site is the possibility that you'll lose your visitors. As a colleague of mine likes to say, "Why on earth would you want to direct people out of your site?" This action is roughly analogous to inviting customers into your store, then telling them they can buy their goods someplace else.

There are several ways of keeping people from jumping ship from your site. One is simply not to include any links that exit your site, a sort of Venus's-flytrap approach that lures people in, then offers them only links leading within the site (flies, however, don't have the luxury of a "Back" button).

Another option is to bury your links in the middle of your site, requiring visitors to explore what you have to offer before they run across any outside links. This can be especially handy if you're involved in reciprocal linking with other sites, as it provides a nesting place for links without giving visitors the chance to bail at the first link they run across (see "Reciprocal Linking" in Chapter 5, *How to Get Links from Hundreds of Sites*).

If these methods sound slightly devious to you, there are other ways to provide outside links while keeping visitors on something of a "loose leash."

Target Windows

Modern Web browsers recognize target tags (see Figure 4-3), which direct your visitor's browser to open the link's destination in a new window, thereby keeping your site in the background.

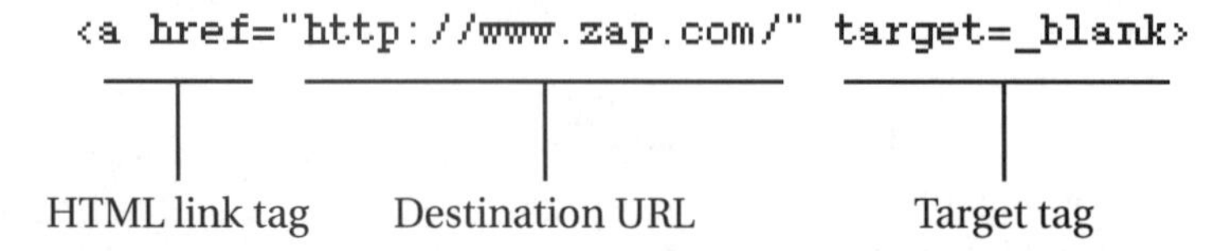

Figure 4–3 Target tags.

If visitors don't like where they've ended up, they can just close the window and be back at your site. If you're savvy with JavaScript, there are ways of specifying the size of the window (so that, for example you can have the other site appear in a smaller window off to the site of your site). You could also create a similar effect using Netscape's frames tags, but those are beyond the scope of this book.

Negotiate Custom Pages

Here's an idea that may take a little more footwork, but it's worth the time. Say your site, French Horns Forever, has a special section devoted to French horn symphonies by J. S. Bach. You don't have the time to research a history of Bach himself, nor to compile a complete list of all his works. However, having that information would be a great addition to your site. Wandering the Web, you've discovered that the Johann Sebastian Bach page `http://www.ukonline.co.uk/UKOnline/Magazine/Music/biogs/js_bach.html` contains a detailed hyperlinked biography of the composer, while the J. S. Bach home page `http://www.tile.net/tile/bach` contains a comprehensive list of Bach's works, complete with recommended recordings.

Contact both site creators, and ask if you can set up a page on their site that says something like, "Welcome visitors from French Horns Forever," with return links to your site. In exchange, you could do the same for them with material from your site; if the new custom page isn't linked from any of your regular pages, only visitors coming from the linked sites will see the custom messages. This technique involves a minimum of work (creating a new HTML file based on existing ones, or even just a banner at the top of the other sites' pages) and most likely won't tax their servers.

The Top 10 Award Sites

When the Web started to get popular, people quickly began to get lost in the multitude of sites, never knowing if they next URL they visited would be worthwhile. Award sites sprang up to highlight the newest, best, or coolest sites available. Although the number of award sites has exploded since then, the following ten award sites consistently draw enormous numbers of visitors each day. They represent a potent sources of visitors—if you're good enough to get listed.

Cool Site of the Day

Cool Site of the Day (CSotD) `http://cool.infi.net` is generally acknowledged as the originator of the "Cool Site" genre. CSotD is also the source of the Cool Site of the Year awards.

Submitting

Click the Submit/Help link, or e-mail cool@infi.net. Include a description of your site, and don't forget to include the URL. "Some really bold people," the site creator writes, "give us a site description and then tell us to use a search engine to find the address. Imagine us laughing before moving on."

Notes

Unlike some award sites, CSotD lists suggestions for what makes a Cool Site of the Day. These include

1. Create something useful.
2. If you can't be useful, be entertaining.
3. Be aware of bandwidth.
4. Think twice about your picture ("Unless 100 people have told you that you're beautiful or remarkable looking, don't put your picture on your Web page").
5. "Surprise us."

Lycos Top 5% of the Web

If you spend much time on the Web without running into a Top 5% icon, check to make sure your modem didn't drop the line. The Lycos Top 5% of the Web site `http://point.lycos.com/categories/index.html` is one of the older and more ubiquitous rating services on the Web.

Submitting

From the main page, click the Help icon or text link. It's a good idea to search for your site in case the Lycos spiders got to it while you weren't looking. If you don't find it in the database, click Add a Site and submit your URL in the field provided.

Notes

As soon as you submit your URL, the Lycos spider grabs the information from your home page and displays a quick rundown for you. Unfortunately, because Lycos receives thousands of URLs per day, there is a two- to four-week delay before your site shows up in the database. Be aware, however, that this process only adds your site to the Lycos database. Lycos's site reviewers determine which sites get added to the Top 5% list.

Too Cool

Too Cool `http://toocool.com`, in addition to selecting a daily Too Cool site, is also a vehicle for the Web design services of its staff. Its daily picks range from slick professional sites like ABC's Monday Night Football `http://www.abcmnf.com` to humorous sites like Premrad `http://www.premrad.com`.

Submitting

A link from the main page, titled Leave-a-Link, seems like the place to submit; but that only takes you to a listing of sites to which anyone can input. To really submit your site for review, click on About Too Cool, then click "mail" under "How does Too Cool find the coolest sites every day?"

Notes

As expected, Too Cool looks for well-designed sites that feature great content. Keep in mind that the creators maintain that they've been offered "many bribes" but so far have "not accepted anything."

Project Cool

After Glenn Davis founded Cool Site of the Day and launched the "cool site" genre, he left it to start Project Cool `http://www/projectcool.com`. In addition to daily Sightings, this site includes Developer Zone (a resource for Web designers) and Future Focus (editorials about the Web, communications, and technology).

Submitting

From the main page, select Sightings, then click Submit a Sighting from the resulting page.

Notes

The Project Cool site is certainly one of the sharpest out there. The information on the site can tend to slant toward Web designers, but the choice of sites doesn't reflect that.

Starting Point

Starting Point `http://www.stpt.com` looks as if it's trying to compete with Yahoo by offering a little bit of everything. The Today's Hot Site is located at the bottom of the page.

Submitting

Click the Submit button in the menu bar and fill in the fields provided. The description field is limited to 512 characters.

Notes

The submission form, in addition to asking for your URL, description, and title, includes an option to have the Starting Point spiders notify you when a similar page is added to their database.

2ask

Sometimes it's not enough to be cool, or be in a top percentage of Web sites. Sometimes you just have to lay claim to being the Best of the Planet. The 2ask site `http://www.2ask.com/` ranks its awards on a global scale, using a 5-star judging system.

Submitting

From the frame at left, click Nominate a Site, then choose from a list of categories that best fits your site. Note that there is also an area where you can review a site if you'd rather write your own review.

Notes

2ask judges according to speed and ease of use, design, quality of content, timeliness, and the level of interactivity and use of technology.

c|net Best of the Web

Megasite c|net's Best of the Web `http://www.cnet.com/Content/Reviews/Bestofweb/index.html` provides a growing collection of sites reviewed by a large team of staff members and freelancers. Reviews are grouped both alphabetically and by category and include a special "Screamer of the Week" section (a highlighted site requiring cutting-edge Web technology).

Submitting

Click Submit Your Favorite Web Site and fill out the fields provided.

Notes

Don't just include your 25-word description in the main field; they're looking for *why* you think the site should be included in their database. Be persuasive. To submit a site, however, you must be a c|net member (which is free).

Cybertown

Cybertown `http://www.cybertown.com/` is an impressive collection of links and resources brought together under a virtual city metaphor. From the main menu, click on the Site of the Week link.

Submitting

e-mail URLs to cybermail@cybertown.com with a request that your URL be added to the list of considered sites.

Notes

Cybertown currently gets about 4 million hits per month. Although the "city" seems on the verge of becoming digital sprawl, you can also find other resources and advertising opportunities.

Netscape's What's Cool

Probably the most-hit What's Cool site on the Web, Netscape's What's Cool page `http:/home.netscape.com/home/whats-cool.html` has the advantage of being a menu item in Netscape's Navigator browser, which currently boasts 60–80% of the browser market. Updated regularly, this page is one of the most highly watched of the "cool" sites.

Submitting

Unfortunately, Netscape no longer appears to accept nominations for sites. Instead, sites are reviewed by the faceless "Netscape cool team." You can, however, look into buying advertising for the page under the Web Site Advertising link.

Notes

Most of the sites on the rotating cool list tend to be big-name sites like United Parcel Service and the *New York Times.* However, interspersed with the heavies are sites like Teen Movie Critic and World Birthday Web.

WebCrawler Top 25

I was hesitant to include WebCrawler's Top 25 list `http://www.webcrawler.com/WebCrawler/Top25.html`, not because it wasn't helpful, but because there's no way to get your site on the list unless it becomes wildly popular. Rather than offer a chosen list of reviewed sites, WebCrawler's Top 25 lists the sites on the Web that are most frequently linked. This does, however, give you some idea of which sites people are visiting; from there, you can contact the site owners to inquire about cross-linking your site.

Web Media

It used to be that if you did something new and noteworthy, you sent a press release or action blurb to your local newspaper and maybe a few magazines. Now, the number of media choices available is staggering. The Web has made it easier and faster to distribute news and information through many emerging electronic magazines ("e-zines") and news services. In this section, I deal with some of the on-line outlets that can get your URL to where people will not only see it, but where they can link directly to it, as well. For detailed information about tailoring your press releases and utilizing traditional media outlets, see Chapter 7, *Producing Hits Offline.*

E-Zines

Electronic magazines have a few big advantages over their printed counterparts. Due to the on-line medium, magazines aren't restricted by length or the fluctuating prices of paper and printing, which means there's less chance of an e-zine cutting your announcement due to lack of space. Also, e-zines can publish whenever they choose: daily, weekly, or sporadically-but-frequently. For you, this means a higher number of locations from which to broadcast your URL. And because sending off a piece of e-mail is faster and less expensive than mailing out a press kit, you can double your output without breaking a sweat (or licking those awful envelope seals).

HotWired

HotWired `http://www.hotwired.com` began as an on-line cousin to *Wired* magazine (which I discuss in Chapter 7) but soon morphed into its own entity, sharing only its attitude, influence, and part of its name with *Wired*. The Net Surf Central section ("the good, the bad, and the utterly useless") spotlights Web sites and offers brief commentary on a daily basis. Contact e-mail editor June Cohen `hotsurf@hotwired.com` to submit your site for review.

NetGuide Live

Like HotWired, NetGuide Live `http://www.netguide.com/gen/page/Home` is an on-line magazine that has ties with a print publication, in this case, *NetGuide*. However, NetGuide Live is not the same site as the Web version of *NetGuide*. Confused yet? This is an example of the often schizophrenic nature of on-line media. However, NetGuide Live is also an example of superior implementation. The SiteGeist section lists new sites and spotlights; NetGuide Live's Best of the Web lists their picks for top sites in a dozen categories, with over 50,000 sites rated and reviewed. Submit your new site's URL to `newsites@netguide.com`; also e-mail The List Guy `listguy@netguide.com`, who groups and presents new sites into subjects.

News Services

Similar to electronic magazines, news services offer news and information about new sites and on-line resources. However, the benefit of using news services is their focus on providing material to editors, writers, and researchers in the media industries. As a result, print and electronic sources get much of their information on Web sites from these services.

Media Central

Updated daily, Media Central `http://www.mediacentral.com` covers all realms of communications, from broadcast and cable to interactive media. You'll want to bookmark this site for your personal use in tracking media trends and getting in-depth profiles and reviews. If you join Media Central, you can receive an e-mail copy of the Media Central Digest every Friday. Contact Marc Perton, Editor-in-Chief mperton@mediacentral.com; Larry Jaffee, Managing Editor ljaffee@mediacentral.com; or Frances Katz, Associate Editor fkatz@mediacentral.com.

Newsbytes

Covering all aspects of the telecommunications, computer, and on-line worlds, Newsbytes http://www.newsbytes.com delivers news releases and data via their Web site or e-mail subscription. Although not as filtered as Media Central, Newsbytes features daily and weekly summaries of its information. Contact Wendy Woods, Editor Wendy_Woods@newsbytes.com.

Success with the Personal Touch

Although the prevalence of spiders, intelligent agents, search engines, and automatically generated forms has drastically increased over the last few years, I try never to let myself believe that the Web has become automatic, like a self-winding clock. Every day I come in contact with the timekeepers and engineers that keep the Web ticking not by mechanics, but by the time they spend online and the words and images they contribute. Put aside the techno-masks and utopian dreams—the Web is more like a thin bed sheet covering its inhabitants than a silicon scaffolding surrounding them.

With the ease and speed of e-mail, the possibilities for connecting with editors and site creators is very great indeed. The best way to develop these impromptu relationships is simply to e-mail people you run across while browsing the Web. Many times I've e-mailed the author of an engaging article or zapped off a note to a designer who has creatively put together a professional site, without needing to hammer my modem into submission. If the person is too busy, or doesn't care, they won't answer—that's the worst that can happen. Usually, though, people will respond, even if only to offer a quick thanks. It's certainly worth taking 30 seconds to write a few-sentence e-mail message.

How does this help you get your site "out there"? Networking is still the best way to influence people—influence them to link to your site, write a column about what you offer on the Web, give your name to others who might be interested in what you have to offer, or point you to resources you hadn't previously considered.

Quality Is One Job (Not Necessarily Job One)

It would be nice just to upload your URL and description in one central location and know that everyone on (and off) the Web would check there daily and flock to your site. It would also be nice if I had a T-1 connection to the Net, but so far I haven't been able to engineer one. Hard work pays big dividends in Web site promotion. By targeting your efforts toward a number of particularly bountiful sources and locations—the ones that will send lots of visitors your way—you'll find that you've saved yourself a lot of time and trouble.

Once your site is in the major search engines and linked from a number of other optimal sites, you've laid the foundation for overheating your server. Now it's time to spread your influence and get the word out en masse. In the next chapter, *Getting Hundreds of Links*, I'll show you how.

5

How to Get Links from Hundreds of Sites

I recently had new business cards printed. I always try to carry a few with me in case I bump into a wealthy software mogul looking for someone to fund. Since the printer's minimum order was 500 cards, I've got plenty to give away—sometimes I hand out two or three at a time. That way, not only do the people receiving my cards possess all the information to reach me—phone number, e-mail, URL, home address—but they can distribute that information to others as well.

Likewise, when others proffer me their cards, I usually ask for more than one. Having multiple copies of cards helps when friends and colleagues ask me for a doctor referral, a favorite restaurant, or where to get a clutch rebuilt—I can simply grab one of the extra cards and pass it along. Because of this, my friends know that I'm a good link to others, specifically, to other people possessing their own set of business cards.

On the Web, the ability to link and cross-link pages works the same way (except it's cheaper, and HTML makes typos easier to fix). The more sites that contain links in my direction, the greater the possibility of generating more hits.

Chapter 4, *How to Get Quality Links*, covered the fine art of tailoring your link selection to produce the best results. In this chapter, I examine the shotgun approach—hitting as many sites as possible over a wide area of interests. I cover some of the benefits and drawbacks of attracting links this way, as well as describing which types of sites can benefit from it. Then I examine the tools available for setting up mass links: announce sites, announce lists, and auto posters. I finish by emphasizing, once again, the advantages of applying a personal touch. We're gunning for everything that moves here, so you might want to wear something orange and reflective while reading through this chapter.

Pros and Cons of Mega Linking

As I mentioned in Chapter 1, *A Million Ways to Get Hits*, the prevailing attitude toward building page impressions favors fewer well-targeted links over numerous disparate ones. However, that doesn't mean you need to focus exclusively on finding that one mythic, best-possible site for your link. Depending on what kind of site you manage, large-scale linking may be an equally good, or even better alternative. Use some of your time garnering links from a broad range of other sites and link lists.

The More the Merrier

In a growing sea of Web sites, having more links in more places increases your chances of bringing people to your site. Some of the most interesting sites I've visited have been the results of following interesting links from otherwise unrelated sites. For example, I never would have stumbled upon *Café Magazine* `http://www.gold.net/users/fy15` if there hadn't been a link to it from *eSCENE, The World's Best Online Fiction* `http://www.etext.org/Zines/eScene`, which I arrived at by way of...well, you get the idea.

The hyperlinked nature of the Web can play to your advantage here: many visitors, unless they're hell-bent on finding something specific, are not immune to the pull of interesting material (for tips on making your site interesting, see Chapter 10, *Refining Your Web Ad Campaign*). Even the most productivity-oriented Web travelers occasionally follow links that promise to lead to entertaining, enlightening, or potentially more useful content. And with the added flexibility built into current Web browsers, a visitor can explore a bit in a new window while still being able to go back to his or her original task in the first window (see Figure 5-1); which makes the temptation to follow interesting-looking links even harder to resist.

Reciprocal Linking

Although I discuss this in more detail in "Barter May Be Better" in Chapter 9, *Launching Your Web Ad Campaign*, let me take the opportunity here to suggest including an extensive links page on your own site. Many sites will agree to include a link to your pages if you create a link to theirs. If you decide to to this route, you may find yourself with an unwieldy, unorganized page of links; however, if the other party hasn't built up a large number of links, your information there will stand out as a boat on the sea, rather than being one of the fish. The reward is certainly worth the time it takes to add one URL to your links page.

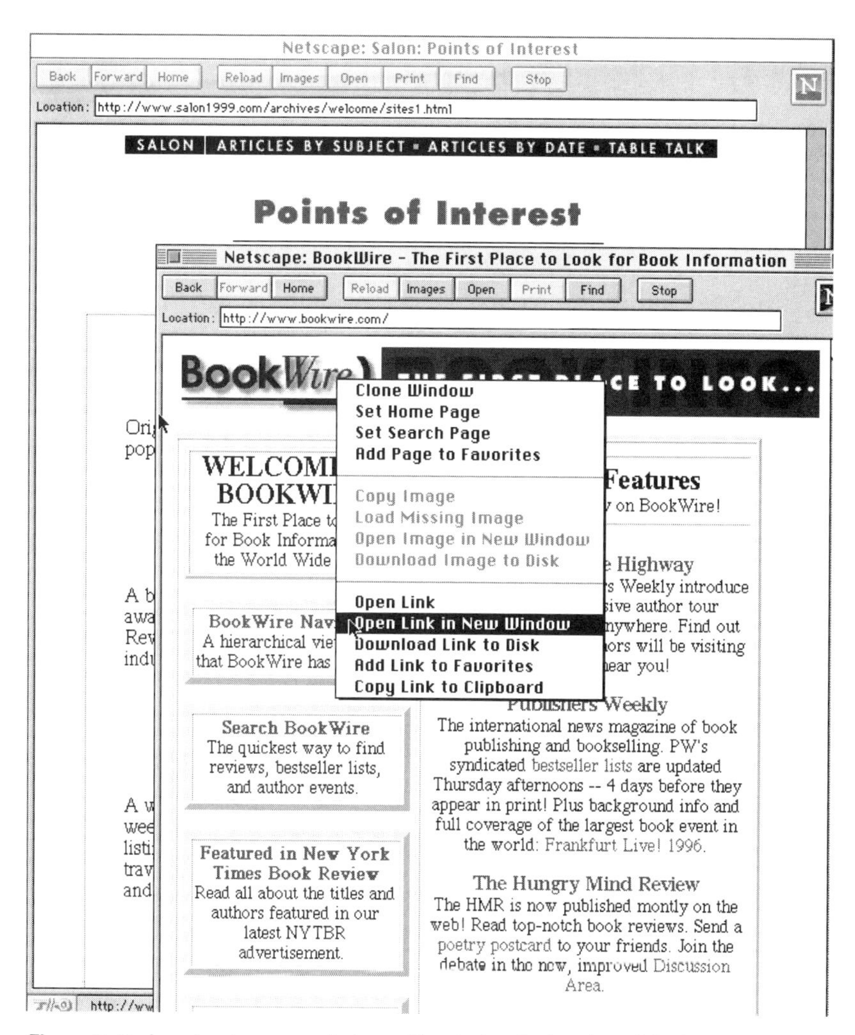

Figure 5–1 Jumping to a new window without abandoning the original.

Benefiting from this Approach

Is large-scale linking the best option for your site? To answer this question, take a look at two factors: your site's content, and the age of your target audience.

Content

General-interest sites that appeal to a wide spectrum of visitors will benefit from large-scale linking. If a lot of people would be attracted to your site—and be honest here; not everyone is interested in polar horticulture—it makes sense to get as many links as possible over a large area.

Does your site fall under the category of entertainment? People will often investigate a link that promises to amuse or enthrall. Some Web creators have discovered that entertainment will even bring visitors to a site whose core content isn't something that would initially provoke a response. Underwear manufacturer JOE BOXER `http://www.joeboxer.com/`, for example, employs a number of amusing techniques to encourage visits, including a page where you can enter a message that will be displayed on JOE BOXER's electronic reader board in New York's Times Square (see Figure 5-2).

Target age

So large-scale linking works for mass-appeal sites. But how do you know if your site has mass appeal? Consider this: research has shown that different age groups use the Web for varying purposes. Entertainment-related sites tend to appeal to younger audiences, who have more time and money to spend online. According to the July 1996 issue of *American Demographics* magazine, users

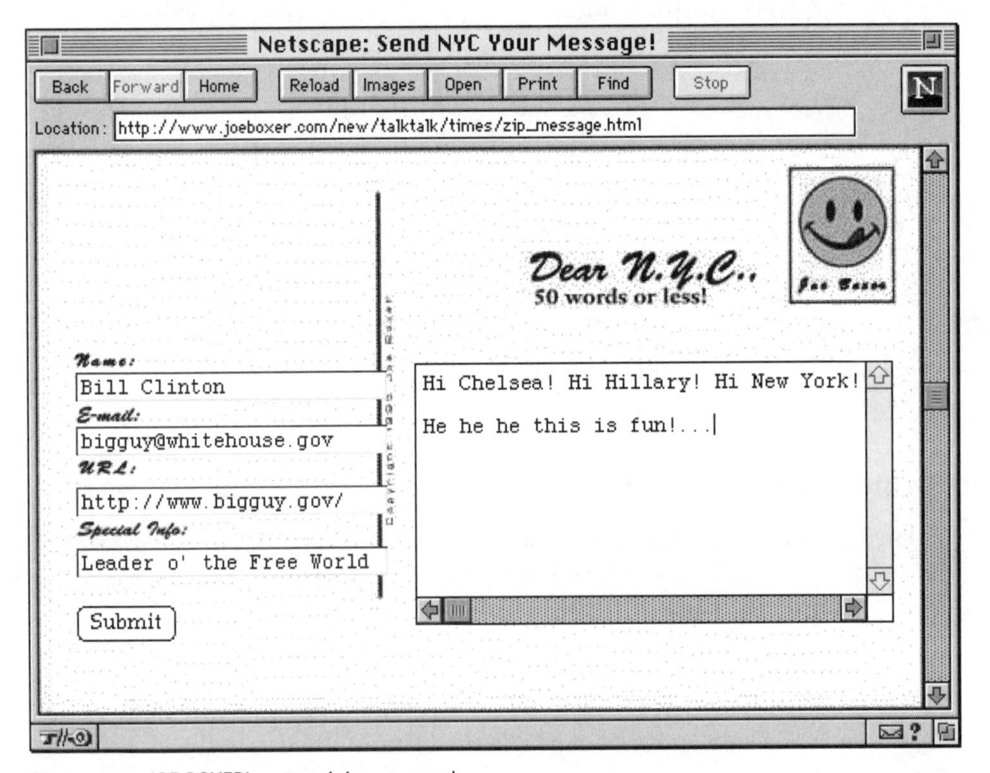

Figure 5-2 JOE BOXER's entertaining approach.

aged 18 to 29 (representing 31% of the total adult audience in the United States) are more likely than their older counterparts to view the Internet as an entertainment vehicle or "personal lifestyle experience." So if you have an entertainment-related site, large-scale linking can connect you to this sizable audience.

Likewise, if your site is more of a content provider, offering news and/or product information, you can take advantage of the large middle-aged (30 to 49) and older (50 and above) brackets, which account for 53% and 13%, respectively, of the adult audience. Knowing which sites appeal to which audiences helps you decide if mass-linking will be beneficial for you.

Potential Drawbacks

There are a couple of potential drawbacks you should keep in mind when trying to accumulate large-scale linking. The first has to do with professionalism: you need to take at least a cursory look at where your URL is going to end up, so that if, for example, you're trying to sell smoked beef jerky over the Web, your URL doesn't appear on the Very Vegetarian list `http://www.cyber-kitchen.com/pgvegtar.htm`.

The second caveat has to do with people's evolving styles of interacting with the Web. Remember that when the Web first started to break into the mainstream, people created link sites which housed nothing but hotlinks to sites of related interests. (In fact, Yahoo began as a bookmark manager and ballooned from there.) Now, with the proliferation of sophisticated search engines, many Web explorers give these huge link lists (many of which can weigh in at 100 to 200K!) only a swift glance before using a search engine to find what they're looking for. In other words, just having your link out there—even on lots of pages—doesn't guarantee that people will see it.

Still tempted to try the mass-linking route? What follows is a summary of tools available to get your links out by the thousands.

Announce Sites

In the early 1990s, the Web as we know it was still a relatively small pond of digital protoplasm. As the Web's popularity increased, however, prehistoric Web surfers clamored to find out what new sites were coming on line, and when. Soon, a few What's New sites emerged from the goo, becoming the prototypes that would evolve into the search engines and directories we're familiar with today. Initially created as no-frills text messages, these announce sites are still—

in cases like Netscape's What's New page—some of the best ways to get your site "out there." Here are a few.

Netscape What's New

Netscape's Navigator is currently the top thunder lizard among Web browsers (its original code name was Mozilla, a 1950s-Japanese-movie fusion of Mosaic and Godzilla), and, because of that, securing a spot on the Netscape What's New page is a coveted position. In what has turned out to be a clever move, Navigator automatically connects to the Netscape home page when it's launched and provides built-in menu items to direct people to the What's New and What's Cool sites. An appearance on Netscape's What's New page practically guarantees a large number of impressions for the lucky few sites that are announced there.

Submission

As of this writing, Netscape appears to have dropped the option of submitting one's site to the What's New page; they are now offering to sell banner advertising space instead. However, it's not entirely clear whether or not the smaller text listings on the What's New page are paid advertisements, or if they have been chosen by members of Netscape's staff. If you're prepared to spend approximately $8,000 to $50,000 for banner advertising, this point is moot; see Chapter 9, *Launching Your Web Ad Campaign*.

What's New Too

In Chapter 2, *How Search Engines Think*, I mentioned that sometimes it can take up to six weeks for a submitted URL to work its way into a search engine's database. Netscape's What's New Too `http://newtoo.manifest.com/WhatsNewToo` processes over 700 new site announcements every day and posts within 36 hours of submission.

Submission

Click Add from the main page to access the What's New Too Submit Page, fill out the form, and click Submit Entry for Preview.

Notes

What's New Too makes it clear at the outset that they will only post a URL once, and that the URL can only fall under one category. Because the service only handles the listings of new files, it's tempting to submit several times per week; however, from the tone of their message, it sounds like they've got a system in place that will filter out duplicate site entries. You can define your site as belonging to one of 17 categories, which are defined on a separate page to help you choose which best suits your site. The description field is set to handle 30 words or less (you've got your 25-word description handy, yes?) and does not accept HTML tags for indicating bolds, italics, and so forth.

InfoSpace

InfoSpace `http://www.infospace.com`, a relative newcomer to the Web, bills itself as "the most innovative directory on the Internet." No information seems to be beyond their grasp; they offer worldwide telephone directories, business directories, government "blue pages," fax numbers, and more. Boosted by an impressive array of licensing and partnership agreements, InfoSpace is a must-add to your link list.

Submission

Choose Submit from the main page.

Notes

The scope of InfoSpace is impressive. Searching for "Don Sellers" in the Accumail section brought up ten results, ranging from Pflugerville, TX, to Hong Kong. Clicking on my name (the correct me) gave me a page of information, including my organization name, address, and phone number. By clicking my address, I was able to view the location on a street-level map (with zooming capabilities), locate nearby businesses, and view a listing of services in the Seattle area that ran the gamut from airlines to video stores. For each service, I was offered, the same options—name, address, phone number, view location, and so on—that I used in my original search. When I clicked on my phone number, the computer played the appropriate touch tones through its speaker, allowing me to dial simply by putting my telephone handset in front of the speaker.

Netsurfer Digest

Netsurfer Digest `http://www.netsurf.com/nsd` is a weekly e-mail newsletter detailing new and interesting news, places, and resources online.

Each issue is e-mailed in either text-only or HTML format and includes brief summaries and descriptions of the featured sites.

Submission

Clicking on The Pressroom brings up a page of information and an e-mail link. Copy one of your prewritten site descriptions into the body of the message, and mail it off.

Notes

The Netsurfer editors write: "As usual, do remember that brevity is the soul of wit. So keep it short, we get hundreds of submissions every week, and the longer they are the less likely it is that we'll look at them." This is another good reason for having prepared descriptions of your site.

NetHappenings

Global Internet's NetHappenings site `http://www.mid.net/NET` not only lets you submit your site information to its daily listing of new and interesting sites, it also includes the ability to search articles by title, keyword, and subject.

Submission

Selecting Net-Happenings Resource Submittal Form calls up a page asking for your e-mail address, site title, URL, category, and description.

Notes

The categories are listed by abbreviated keywords, so take a moment to decipher them by clicking Keyword Category above the list. Although some are self-explanatory (BOOK), others can be confusing at first (like CONF-NA for Conferences-North America, SEM for Seminars, and JEWEL, which wasn't listed in the descriptions).

comp.infosystems.www.announce

The Usenet newsgroup comp.infosystems.www.announce is a moderated group that posts messages about new Web resources, sites, and site changes. For more information about newsgroups, see Chapter 6, *Mining the Hidden Gold in Mailing Lists and Newsgroups*.

Submission

Announcements can be posted directly to the newsgroup or e-mailed to the moderator at `www-announce@boutell.com`.

Notes

Read the Frequently Asked Questions (FAQ) file! It's posted twice-weekly on the newsgroup and contains specific instructions on how to format, label, and post your announcement. Important tip: the moderator of the newsgroup does not accept commercial advertising or posts that convey information of only local interest.

Nerd World What's New

Although its name suggests a wealth of computer geek-related items, Nerd World `http://www.nerdworld.com/whatsnew.html` is actually a fairly large subject index and search engine. Receiving over one million views per month, this What's New page just might make you carry your scientific calculator with more pride.

Submission

After familiarizing yourself with the categories available, choose Submit Link and fill out the information fields.

Notes

It's necessary to scan the categories and topics here, because the Category list on the submission page goes on forever. Also, be sure to read the guidelines specifying description length, HTML markup, and so on. Note that Nerd World has a two-month backlog on average of links to be added; a Preferred Link option is available, but it involves a fee.

Internet Link Exchange

A fairly new spin on generating visits is the practice of link exchanges. Essentially, link exchange is based on the tried-and-true bartering system, where you agree to run a friend's banner and he runs yours. With link exchanges, however, the transaction process is done for you by an exchange company. Here's how it works.

- You insert a few lines of HTML code into your Web page that look something like this. (Example from the Internet Link Exchange):

```
<center>
<a href="http://ad.linkexchange.com/1/X001000/gotoad.map"
target="_top">
<img width=440 height=40 border=1 ismap
  alt="Internet Link Exchange"
  src="http://ad.linkexchange.com/1/X001000/logoshowad?
  free"></a><br>
<font size=1>
<a href="sponsors.html">Please Visit Our Sponsors</a>
</font>
<p>
```

- When someone accesses your page, your HTML file directs their browser to go retrieve a banner ad from a link exchange member's server, which will then appear on your page.
- The link exchange company keeps track of how often the banner appears on your Web site, then credits you with points that apply toward free banner advertisements of your own on other members' sites. The exchange company gets it money from donations and sponsorships.

So far, the Internet Link Exchange `http://www.linkexchange.com/` is the primary exchange company operating on the Web. In addition to operating as outlined above, the ILE provides up-to-the-minute statistics on visits, click-throughs, and the number of times a banner is displayed, and a display to click ratio. If you don't have a banner, or want to make sure your sites are designed effectively, free banner creation services are also available.

To submit, click the About/Join button at ILE's main page. You will be presented with a list of terms and conditions that you must agree to in order to proceed, after which you fill out the form that appears. There are several questions dealing with your site's potential categories, and others regarding the level of the rating system at which you wish to classify yourself (level one is intended for children only, while level three roughly corresponds to a "PG-13" movie rating).

Let the Auto Poster Do It

Someone, no doubt frustrated by the number of times they had to retype their Web site information into each search engine's Add URL fields, came up with the bright idea to tie together the main search engines' submittal forms in one neat package. Now several such packages, called auto posters, exist. The best of these, like Submit-It, only require you to type the information in once; the info is then distributed to other sites. Other auto posters provide a number of forms that comply with different search engines' custom fields. And still others provide lists of links directly to search engines' Add URL forms. A brief rundown of some auto posters follows.

Submit-It

I mentioned Submit-It in Chapter 3, *Making Search Engines Do Your Bidding*. Submit-It reminds me of my pasta machine at home. I can make fresh pasta with a minimum of fuss in the time it takes to boil the water to cook it in, because the machine's designers had idiots in mind when they designed it. That's not to say I'm an idiot in the kitchen—it's just a good example of something that does its job well because it was designed to operate for absolutely anyone. (With my pasta machine, if you don't have all the parts on correctly, the motor won't even engage.) Submit-It requires that you type your contact information once. When you're done, it returns a page with submission buttons to 18 prominent search engines and directories—with each form already filled out. All you have to do is verify the information and click the respective Submit buttons.

Submit-It also offers Gold and Pro versions of its service, which are fee-based and cost up to $300.

PROFESSIONAL HELP

Here's something important to keep in mind: as with many Web-related activities, the response once you've submitted your URL to an auto poster will take longer than you expect. You still have to deal with the transmission times to the various search engines, as well as the copying and pasting (or typing, if you're into self-inflicted pain) process. Don't expect to blast your presence onto the Net in an hour or so. Depending on how much time you have available, you may wish to consider hiring a company to not only fill out all the submission forms, but also (if they're good) to get your URL to the many places that slip between the cracks of the big auto posters. See "Web Publicists" in Chapter 11, *The Benefits of Professional Help*.

PostMaster2

PostMaster2 `http://www.netcreations.com/postmaster` is primarily a commercial site, with a "try before you buy" option that allows you to post to several main search engines. You must register with their system before you can submit to anything. However, they have the capability to submit to 417 search engines, directories, and media outlets, in addition to 1,585 "interested individuals." Even if you choose not to go through the "buy" route, you can still download search engine software and other information about promoting your site.

WebStep Top 100

WebStep `http://www.mmgco.com/top100.html` offers 100 free sites and search engines to which to submit your information, with a short description of each to help you choose which ones will benefit the most from your announcement. The list is updated frequently, so be sure to refer to it when you're out checking to ensure that your links got placed.

Higher Saturation with Announce Lists

Even the best auto posters are limited in scope, due to the size of the Web and the varieties of methods that sites use to enter information. To make sure your site saturates the nooks and crannies of the Web, you'll want to explore the following link lists. Essentially, the creators of these lists have provided you with scores of hotlinks that go directly to search engines' submission forms. So, while you still have your work cut out for you in fully promoting your site, these lists at least allow you to bypass the process of trolling the Web for places to which to submit your information.

The Internet Promotions Megalist

You want links? Have at 'em! The Megalist `http://www.2020tech.com/submit.html` includes links to What's New services, search engines, Usenet newsgroups, Web sites that require reciprocal links, and an array of specialized sites ranging from Africa-related to Women-specific sites. To help you out, the creators of the Megalist have marked "very important Internet resources" with stars.

The Green Eggs Report

The Green Eggs Report `http://ibd.ar.com/ger` takes an unusual approach to collecting URLs. Rather than build a spider that traverses the Web, indexing pages as it crawls, the Green Eggs' Rumor Database System perches on the edge of the Usenet spool, grabbing URLs from messages that are posted to newsgroups. To link your site to this directory, just post a message to a newsgroup that includes your URL.

Go Net-Wide

Organized alphabetically, Go Net-Wide `http://www.shout.net/~whitney/html/gopublic.html` provides links to over 100 sites, including unusual ones like Sherlock Holmes Links, The URL Centrifuge, and several variations of cybermalls.

announce.net

Announce.net `http://www.announcenet.com` offers direct links to 35 What's New pages, including regulars like Yahoo and Alta Vista, as well as less-common sites like What's New in Japan, New WAIS Resources, and New Spots to Shop. Clicking on any of the links under See What's New on the Net takes you to the What's New pages.

The Personal Touch

Although I brought up the importance of using a personal touch in Chapter 4, *How to Get Quality Links*, I must emphasize it once again here. As you've probably realized, using a personal touch in your Web interactions works with many facets of the Web.

If you're exploring the Web in your spare time (or in the time you sneak in between meetings and market research), it doesn't hurt to send brief e-mails to site creators asking them if they're interested in trading links. Because you're approaching them on a one-to-one basis, they probably won't make a fuss about considering your offer. The fine art of letter-writing may be a fading discipline, but the age of the zapped-off e-mail is now in full swing. Just don't blatantly waste their time by sending what is obviously a prefabricated marketing appeal.

It takes a bit of work and effort to get your site's URL and information to places on the Web where the people you want to find it will do so. After having my business cards printed, the worst thing I could have done would have been to leave them in the box where no one would see them. It takes effort to make yourself known to the right people, but experience has shown me that it pays off—usually sooner than I expect.

Now that you've blanketed a sizable portion of the Web with your digital business cards, it's time to look into another approach to attracting visitors—through mailing lists and newsgroups.

6

Mining the Hidden Gold in Mailing Lists and Newsgroups

Before the Internet was available to the general public, I was a member of CompuServe and frequented its subject-based discussion groups, called forums. One day, I produced a brilliant idea that I wanted to post; I felt its appeal was so universal that I should post it in various discussion groups, even though the message didn't fall into the subject matter of any one forum. I posted to four forums: One ignored me. From another I received an interested response. From the third I received two curt messages saying I shouldn't be posting there, as the subject material was not appropriate. In the last I was viciously attacked by a number of participants, equating me with Hitler, Stalin, and Nero. Strangely, that group was CompuServe's Humor Forum, though there was no humor in their replies. I was able to mollify the forum after I explained the reasoning behind my posting (with a few jokes thrown in); however, the entire exercise proved to be a vexing waste of time.

If you think the people on CompuServe's Humor Forum were vicious, you should see what happens when you try to post off-subject messages in some current mailing lists and newsgroups. Mailing lists (e-mail-based discussion groups) and newsgroups (bulletin board-like discussion groups arranged under the umbrella of Usenet) can be bountiful venues for site promotion. These groups often contain a very specific membership that may fit your target audience perfectly. Members of discussion groups tend to be experts and opinion makers in a particular field, making them valuable contacts for the promoter.

On the other hand, discussion groups have their own history and sociology. One cannot simply blunder into a group without running the risk of offending a member—someone who may be the very person you want to befriend. Like mining gold, you may receive great payoffs from a discussion group; but it's also dangerous work. This chapter will show you how to maximize the gain and minimize the risk in working with these groups. First I delve into the sociology of mailing lists and newsgroups. Then I provide insights and tools on how to find the appropriate discussion group in which to promote. Finally I discuss the right and wrong ways to promote your site.

The on-line community has volunteers who have generously created resources to help new users understand the nuances of posting to mailing lists and newsgroups. At various places in this chapter I recommend you read particular sources in newsgroups or on the Web. Please check these sources out, as there is nothing like getting information directly from discussion group pros to make you comfortable with and adept at the process.

Mailing List and Newsgroup Backgrounder

Because the Web has grown so rapidly, many people have come to on-line life without a knowledge or appreciation of the tried-and-true ways in which people use computers share information. Both mailing lists and newsgroups act as mechanisms where people can meet, share information, discuss topics, and generally promote the increase and dissemination of knowledge.

As I describe below, mailing lists and newsgroups differ in function, but they have much in common regarding how they should be approached and handled. Both of these types of discussion venues were originated by bright and technically proficient people. These early members developed ways to communicate effectively and productively that are now tacitly agreed upon by the discussion group communities. Understanding the different histories of mailing lists and newsgroups helps you interact with them.

Mailing Lists

Mailing lists are the offspring of networks and e-mail. People who sent e-mail to one another would often copy messages and forward them to others who might be interested. These users realized that the forwarding method was an inefficient, haphazard way to provide an interested group with information. So the mailing list was born. The idea was that one would subscribe to a mailing list on some subject, say stress fracture analysis. Then one could send e-mail to the list and the list's server would distribute that e-mail to all of the people who had subscribed.

All mailing lists have administrators; in the early days, the administrator manually entered people on and removed people from the distribution lists, answered inquiries, and performed general maintenance. Nowadays, modern mailing list software, such as the popular LISTSERV, handles most of these mundane chores without human intervention. However, human administrators still oversee the process. Most modern mailing lists have three e-mail addresses that are important to you: the automated list server's address, which you use to subscribe, get information, and cancel your subscription; the list address, to which you send the messages that will be distributed to others on the list; and the list administrator, who can be contacted on those rare occasions when the system doesn't seem to be working correctly.

Modern mailing lists can be categorized in two broad areas: private vs. public and moderated vs. nonmoderated. Public lists, as the name implies, allow anyone to join. Membership on a private list only is dependent on your fulfilling some requirement, which can vary from professional qualifications to acceptance by the other members. Moderated lists, again as the name implies, have a moderator, who acts as a message gatekeeper. The moderator reads submitted messages and sends on only those deemed acceptable. The moderator may also edit messages and produce a digest of messages on the list. Messages to nonmoderated lists go to all the subscribers, whether the content makes sense or not.

Mailing lists first became popular on ARPANET, a large, expensive network that initially connected organizations involved in United States government research to one another. Over time ARPANET grew to give access to the staff and students of universities and colleges; later it spread internationally. Ultimately, ARPANET evolved into the Internet, there are now tens of thousands of mailing lists publicly available to anyone having e-mail access to the Net.

Newsgroups

Newsgroups began with modems. They grew out of a need for computer users who were not connected to large networks to exchange information on subjects of mutual interest. In 1979, a small group of computer specialists at Duke University and the University of North Carolina developed a UNIX-based system in which computers would call each other on the phone, exchange information via a 300 baud modem, and disconnect. The information they exchanged involved discussions on specific subjects (initially all about UNIX), but as time went on and more and more computers became part of the system, other subject areas were added.

Netnews, as it was then called, was described by its originators as a "as rapid access newsletter." Netnews users could exchange information in a configuration that was much cheaper and easier to set up than a connection to ARPANET, so the two systems grew separately. Netnews became Usenet, which is the hard-to-define umbrella of user-controlled conventions determining how the newsgroups function. Although many people can now access Usenet newsgroups via ARPANET's descendant, the Internet, newsgroups don't need the Internet to exist, as its devotees will quickly tell you.

Usenet contains thousands of subject-delineated newsgroups in which messages are posted by users. Each site that accesses Usenet (for example, an Internet service provider) determines which newsgroups will be available to its users. As a result, newsgroups considered obscure or offensive may not be carried. If you can read a message posted to a newsgroup, you can post your own—but some newsgroups are moderated, so your message may have to win the moderator's acceptance.

Because of its history, most notably regarding the lack of individual administration or moderation of most newsgroups, Usenet is often described as anarchy. Usenet newsgroups tend to be self-policing, and the community has developed methods of dealing with aberrant behavior. Often these methods involve flames (hostile messages) or even more unpleasant repercussions, such as overloading the offender's server. But like mailing lists, if you approach newsgroups with respect, they can be extremely valuable for exchanging information and telling people about your site.

Usenet contains well over 15,000 newsgroups (how many there are depends on your definition of Usenet). As with mailing lists, the first trick to promoting in a newsgroup is to determine in which of the thousands of groups you should post.

Identifying Appropriate Targets

The need is simple: You want to identify newsgroups and mailing lists used by people who might be interested in visiting your site. Unfortunately, there is no one easy way to search through all mailing lists and newsgroups. But some very good and easy-to-use aids in finding most appropriate discussion groups do exist.

Mailing List Directories

The Web itself contains resources to help solve the historic problem of finding mailing lists: those Web sites that function as mailing list directories. Unfortunately, none of these sites has a comprehensive list, and none ever will. Mailing lists, by their nature, remain private unless someone decides to disseminate the information about them. And sometimes their members choose to keep them quiet.

I include the best mailing list directories, below. For other mailing list directories and more information about mailing lists, check out the Yahoo site `http://www.yahoo.com/Computers_and_Internet/Internet/Mailing_Lists`.

Liszt

Liszt `http://www.liszt.com` is to mailing lists what a spider index search engine is to the Web. Liszt uses a spider that checks servers to see if they host mailing lists; if so, Liszt collects information on the mailing list in the Liszt database. Mailing lists can also be submitted directly to Liszt, if the spider hasn't picked them up in its travels.

When you search through Liszt, the search results are color coded so that you can see how much information Liszt has on each mailing list. Liszt often provides help on finding further information on a list, including how to join it. Although Liszt's database holds thousands of mailing lists, the directory is by no means comprehensive. Liszt is a good place to start, but you will probably want to check out some of the other directories to make a complete search.

Reference.COM

Reference.COM `http://www.reference.com` principally acts as a giant archive of messages from publicly accessible mailing lists and newsgroups. The archive provides sophisticated search tools to help you quickly hone in on messages in various discussion groups. This capability alone would make Reference.COM a great Web resource, but, besides searching for messages, Reference.COM is also capable of searching for particular mailing lists or newsgroups themselves. Reference.COM's large database often yields more search results—sometimes significantly more—than the other directories listed here.

PAML

PAML (Publicly Accessible Mailing Lists) `http://www.neosoft.com/internet/paml` may not have the largest database nor the sexiest of interfaces, but it conveys the most human touch of these directories, so it is worth a mention here. You can search for mailing lists by name or subject keyword.

CataList

CataList `http://www.lsoft.com/lists/listref.html` is maintained by L-Soft, the producer of the LISTSERV software that manages mailing lists. CataList enables you to search for publicly accessible mailing LISTSERV lists, and it sometimes contains mailing lists missed by the others.

Newsgroup Directories

A search for newsgroups may be a bit more difficult than one for mailing lists, because fewer resources exist to help you out. Here are three ways to find them: Reference.COM, Deja News, or a self-search through your own listing of newsgroups. You may also want to check out Yahoo's newsgroup information and links `http://www.yahoo.com/News/Usenet`.

Reference.COM

Reference.COM `http://www.reference.com` maintains a database of over 18,000 newsgroups through which you can search. Unfortunately, you may discover some perfect newsgroups to which your service provider does not subscribe. In that case, contact your site administrator and request that the newsgroup be added. The administrator will often be glad to comply.

Deja News

Deja News `http://www.dejanews.com` has over 120 gigabytes of indexed and archived Usenet messages, extending back to March of 1995. You can use the sophisticated search engine in Deja News to search for and read Usenet messages as part of a wide search for potential newsgroups to post to. Deja News also includes a newsgroup posting service through which you can post to Usenet directly from the Deja News site.

Self Search

Most software that accesses Usenet newsgroups offers the capability of searching through a list of all the newsgroups subscribed to by your site. You may have to search for abbreviations or variations on keywords—and you may have to get creative in keyword selection—but you can usually find most of the appropriate sites very easily yourself. Some search engines, such as Alta Vista `http://www.altavista.digital.com` and HotBot `http://www.hotbot.com`, allow you to search Usenet messages.

Approaches that Work

So now you've unearthed a number of mailing lists and newsgroups with a readership that might be interested in your Web site. How do you proceed from here? A number of strategies are available to you. Promotion in discussion group messages runs from direct pitches, where your entire content blatantly touts your site, all the way to a single mention of your URL in your signature. Where you fall on the spectrum depends on the expectations of the discussion group and how much time and effort you want to spend determining the best approach.

In this section I discuss the best method for initially observing potential groups, the best way to write a message, and the best approach to packaging your promotional message so it will be most palatable to potential groups. In the next section, "Strike Outs to Avoid," I discuss some of the common pitfalls encountered by beginners. Further valuable information can be obtained from "Primer on How to Work With the Usenet Community" by Chuq Von Rospach in news.misc or `http://www01.ny.us.ibm.net/userinfo/uuprimer.html`, and "Advertising on Usenet How to Do It," by Joel K. Furr in news.announce.newusers or at `http://www.danger.com/advo.html`.

Reconnaissance

When it comes to understanding how a group works, there is no substitute for lurking. Lurking, the process of reading a group's messages without posting any of your own, is an old and respected on-line tradition. Join the mailing list or read the newsgroup every day to see how the community interacts. You will see others whose messages include their URLs. How do others respond to these messages?

For newsgroups, you can also try to find the group's charter or FAQ (Frequently Asked/Answered Questions). Generally, both are periodically posted in the newsgroups themselves, but you can also search for FAQs at `http://www.cis.ohio-state.edu/hypertext/faq/usenet/top.html`. Some newsgroups will not have this information available.

Netiquette

When I am driving, I sometimes make rude remarks to other drivers. I realize that such behavior suggests a deficient psychological foundation, but I know I am not alone. Many people act as if the normal social contract of consideration for others no longer applies when one is behind the wheel. The physical insulation afforded by the car seems to promote this antisocial behavior.

On-line communication also suffers from physical insulation, with similar results. Devoid of subtle hints of voice tone and inflection and the signals of body language, on-line postings are often misunderstood and overreacted to. These conflicts arise so often that the on-line community has developed "netiquette," a set of conventions and customs designed to minimize friction and maximize communication.

A good foundation in netiquette can be gleaned from The Net: User Guidelines and Netiquette by Arlene H. Rinaldi `http://rs6000.adm.fau.edu/rinaldi/netiquette.html`. The basic premise of netiquette is that on-line discussions involve communication with real live people, not with the insulating keyboard and monitor you use to write to them. Keep these netiquette basics in mind when posting a message to a discussion group:

- Make your titles short and descriptive.
- Keep your writing brief and to the point.
- Watch your spelling and grammar.
- Remember that sarcasm and humor are misinterpreted easily, so you need to let people know when you have your tongue in your cheek.
- When responding to another message, summarize the text you're responding to or respond directly to the sender, not to the group.
- Watch the hype. Discussion group participants are often experts in their fields and usually resent unfounded claims.
- Think twice before you write something derogatory about someone.

For further points on how to write a net-friendly letter, check out `http://www.cs.ubc.ca/spider/edmonds/usenet/good-newgroup.html`.

Your Site in a Sugar Wrapper

If you've checked out a discussion group and found that an obvious promotional piece is acceptable, go ahead and post one. However, you will probably find that most discussion groups resent blatant self promotion. But don't despair of attaining discussion group promotion; your URL *will* generally be welcome, *if* it is included within a meaningful message.

Here's an example posted by Steve Roth of Thunder Lizard Productions in the Online Advertising mailing list.

re: Tony Hsieh's posting:

>We compare some of the click-thru ratios of banners that we have tested >to advertise our service, the Internet Link Exchange. Each banner has >been shown over 16,000 times, so we believe the results to be statistically >significant.

As a direct-mail marketer, we're incredibly interested in statistical significance (and click-through rate). If we mail 10,000 pieces and get a one-percent response rate, what will we get on the next mailing?

I've put up a little Excel spreadsheet on our Web site that calculates statistical significance (we hired a UW math student to create it for us). http://www.thunderlizard.com/misc/statsign.html

Hope you find this useful! It should be equally valid for banner-impressions versus clicks.

Steve has something relevant to the current discussion that he is willing to give to the list subscribers; all they have to do is go to his site to get it. Of course, one can expect that many of these visitors, all very interested in Internet Marketing, might also notice the Web advertising conference Steve is promoting at the same site. But none of them would resent the connection, because they are receiving something valuable for the visit.

Even your e-mail signature can be a precious source of referrals to your site. As long as your postings show you as a contributing member of the discussion, your readers will see your signature and check out your site often, especially if the signature highlights the URL and explains your site's function.

Strike Outs to Avoid

Although on-line discussion groups have only existed for a relatively short period of time, some mistakes are so common that they act as triggers to turn off the members of the group. In the best of all possible worlds, the established members of a discussion group would forgive the follies of newer posters, remembering their own early days. But, unfortunately, some hot buttons will make old-timers grimace as they press their delete keys. If you want a comprehensive (and funny) treatise on what not to do, read Dear Emily Postnews by Brad Templeton in the Usenet newsgroup news.announce.newusers. But keep in mind that it's a satire.

Blatant Self Service

Discussion groups work on the premise that people freely give information to others in the group so that all will benefit. Lurkers are tolerated because they are invisible, don't detract from the process, and yield valuable understanding of the group's process to newcomers. But what if a member keeps posting notices that will only benefit him or her? Such self service cuts against the grain of the entire discussion process and will quickly be resented.

Tone Deafness

The point of lurking is to develop a sense of what's acceptable and what's not in a discussion group. But some people refuse to accept the idea of fitting into an established discussion community. "The Internet is a free place," they say. "No one is going to tell me how to act." In fact, all sorts of people will instantly tell you how to act, if you annoy them sufficiently. Because discussion groups form a community, they act like any human community: they are accepting of people who appear like them and suspicious of people who don't. If you want to act contrary to what you know is acceptable behavior, be my guest; just keep in mind that the suspicion will be there, too.

Spamming

Spamming refers to the process of arbitrarily mailing messages to large numbers of people. By definition, the overwhelming majority of people who receive spamming don't want it—it is an intrusion on their lives and sometimes their wallets. However, those who have the same philosophy of marketing as the people who call me during dinner each night probably think spamming makes perfect sense.

The seminal case of Internet spamming occurred early in 1994. Laurance Canter and Martha Siegel, two partners in a Phoenix law firm, used a program to mail out a message containing information on a Green Card lottery to as many Usenet newsgroups as possible. The magnitude of this act so enraged some members of the on-line community that the mail server used to send the messages was electronically attacked, rendering it inoperable. Postings were made with reproductions of seemingly genuine court transcripts describing the unpleasant reasons why Laurance Canter had permanently left the Florida bar in 1988. At the same time, antispam filters were quickly developed to prevent this type of spamming from occurring again. Carter and Siegel actually benefited from the spamming (see Chapter 8, *Advertising Overview*), so some people still view the process favorably. Just remember: if you want to spam, you do so at your peril.

Technical Deficiency

None of us is perfect. For example, I often forget to inactivate my signature when I am mailing to mailing list servers, which is no big deal, except I then get an automatic reply because the mailing list processor tried to understand my signature as a command and couldn't make sense out of it. I should know better.

Technical errors can reveal us to be technically deficient, a quality often disdained in discussion groups whose members have a high degree of technical expertise. In a recent example, a mailing list I subscribe to sent me 10 messages from the same fellow, each one having the same title. But all of the messages had different contents. Such odd behavior makes the reader pause and perhaps assume that the sender didn't know what he was doing. Try to keep in mind what the subscribers will be seeing when they receive your messages.

No act will label you as a cretin as quickly as if you send a command to the mailing list rather than the list's server. The list server will have an address like listserv@host, listproc@host, or majordomo@host. If you send the message UNSUBSCRIBE to the list itself, those subscribers who are tolerant will realize all of us make mistakes; the others, however, won't.

7

Producing Hits Offline

URLs appear all over the place: on the sides of busses, on frozen vegetable packages, in ferry schedules. But I see them mostly in article after article in magazines. Off-line references to your URL can yield a big jump in site visits, and a strong recommendation in the right place can lead to serious server strain. With the appropriate approach you can often obtain the inclusion of your URL in publications such as magazines, books, and CDs. You can also use media directly under your control, such as business cards and stationery, to get your URL into other people's hands and minds.

Publication Announcements, Step One: The Press Release

The foundation of contacting the press is the press release, which I suggested you write in Chapter 1, *A Million Ways to Get Hits*. Sometimes you can get great review of your site in a publication by just sending a press release with a simple cover letter. But the press release usually represents just the starting point of a successful off-line promotional campaign. You can often bolster your effort by building a personal relationship with publishers, journalists, editors, reviewers—anyone who may get your URL out to the public. Most often your success will depend on your level of effort, but not always—some magazines may just not have a place for you, even though you've befriended an editor.

You may find you have to tailor both the release and your cover letter to a particular publication and/or section within that publication. You will usually use press releases when promoting to both magazines and books, and you need to wield them correctly. You can do so if you keep the following points in mind.

Target Your Material

Nothing drives hardworking journalists mad as quickly as receiving press releases about a subject that doesn't fit their publication. Tailor your information to the particular venue: make sure your material covers what you want to say, and don't forget to include the requisite site and contact information. On the one hand, your promotional material should be concise; on the other, press releases often serve as the basis for entire reviews, so the journalist must have enough information to work with. Don't send press releases or material about minor events like promotions, office relocations, and so forth.

Take the Right Approach

Determine the appropriate contact at the publication. Don't send more than one query to a publication, unless you feel there are two areas that might use it. If so, mention in your cover letter that you sent a release to the other fellow, too. Many magazines have lead times of three months or more, so make sure you have your material in well before any event you are promoting. Here's the biggest no no: don't make a follow up call. If journalists want to call you, they will.

Now that you have the basics of good press relations, I will look at the magazines and books that may serve as valuable promotional vehicles. Following that, I'll discuss how to promote your URL in your day-to-day business publications and activities.

Magazines

You only have to sashay into any large bookstore or newspaper stand to see the overwhelming abundance of Internet-related magazines currently available. When sending your press release or promotional information to a magazine, bear in mind that you are contacting journalists who are probably overworked. Therefore, you will score big points if they get the impression you want to make their job easier. Take the time to buy the magazine, tear off the plastic wrap, throw out the AOL or GNN disc, and look through to get a sense of the magazine's tone and style. Which columns or writers look like they might cover your site? You'll stand a better chance of success if you contact those relevant sources directly.

Magazines fall into two broad categories: those that cover the Internet, and those that target specific subjects that are similar to your site. Keep both types in mind when developing your campaign.

Internet-related

Yahoo's listing of Internet-related magazines `http://www.yahoo.com/Business_and_Economy/Products_and_Services/Magazines/Computers/Internet/` provides a good starting point for building a slate of potential targets. I discuss some of the more popular Internet magazines below; if you can get your URL mentioned favorably in any of these, your server is sure to get hot for a while. However, some of the lesser-known magazines, while yielding fewer hits, may be easier to get your site address into.

Not surprisingly, all of these magazines have associated Web sites; sometimes they are *so* associated that one may have a difficult time determining where the print magazine ends and an on-line version starts.

Internet World

Internet World `http://www.iw.com`, an established, authoritative magazine for Internet users, includes Web sites in some of its stories but is far from a URL-every-other-line grab bag. As the magazine puts it, "We rarely if ever review Web sites. Occasionally one will be mentioned in the Surfboard section if it's particularly offbeat. Most of the time, however, sites are mentioned in the context of an article, not as a standalone review."

Hearing that statement, one may think that *Internet World* doesn't seek site information. Quite the opposite is true, and the magazine should be applauded for their sensible, honest, and straightforward approach to helping promoters contact them. Visit *Internet World*'s Press Release Page at `http://www.iw.com/pr/index.shtml`. There you'll find some salient points on how you can put your best foot forward with your press release. More important, this page lists the topics covered in upcoming issues (about three months out) and solicits announcements for *Internet World*'s News section. Very elegant and worth a monthly check.

If you've read the magazine and just know they need to publish your URL, try contacting Senior Editor Andrew Kantor `ak@iw.com`. If you feel the Surfboard section cannot live without mentioning your site, you can contact Eric Berlin or Andrew Kantor at `surf@iw.com`. You'll be ahead of the game if your site is clever, outrageous, unusual, or groundbreaking (or a combination of all four).

NetGuide

NetGuide `http://techWeb.cmp.com/ng/home/main/` covers a wide range of Web issues for designers, surfers, managers, lurkers, you name it. More effusive with subject matter and URLs than Internet World, NetGuide covers the breadth of Web issues, from HTML tips to financial sites to modems. If you don't know where your URL should go in the magazine, send your press release to `pressrel@netguide.cmp.com`.

NetGuide's Maximum Impact section, to which a number of their editors contribute, looks at a variety of sites and the people behind them. This isn't just a surf column, but more of an in-depth investigation of a site's essence: who's behind it, why it exists, and who the typical visitor is. If Maximum Impact seems right for you, try contacting one of the senior editors, Judith H. Bernstein `jbernste@cmp.com` or Kate Gerwig `kgerwig@cmp.com`, or Associate Editor Kathleen Sands `ksands@cmp.com`.

Yahoo! Internet Life

Yahoo! Internet Life `http://www.yil.com` wants give you the impression that they are *Wired* put out by high school students, but, in reality, this magazine has a good deal of content. Neither the editorial staff nor the writers take themselves too seriously, and you can hardly turn a page without tripping over a passel of URLs. Such a rich profusion of site references makes finding the right editor important. Send new site announcements to Editorial Assistant Elissa Klotz `elissa_klotz@zd.com`. Otherwise, browse through the magazine, see which columnist might be interested in your site, and send that person a note. The staff list is available at `http://www.zdnet.com/yil/content/misc/staff.html`. If you still can't determine who to target, try Senior Editor Elisabeth Holzer `eholzer@zd.com`.

Wired

Wired `http://www.hotwired.com/wired`, the premier magazine covering the Internet, will be a long shot for most sites, but you never know. *Wired* sprinkles a few URLs in its feature articles, but the nuggets increase substantially in the Street Cred and Net Surf sections.

Street Cred singles out notable books, music, and Web sites for capsule reviews. Where appropriate, Street Cred lists a URL at the bottom of an article. If you want to be considered for inclusion in Street Cred, send your press release or other submission material to `streetcred@wired.com`.

Net Surf (which usually follows Street Cred) includes a jumble of sites and Web explorations sometimes loosely tied together by a common theme. Featured sites are given a short review.

Wired hangs its on-line hat as one of the many sections of hotwired.com. HotWired provides a robust selection of useful tools, information, and entertainment for the Web surfer; however, there's a dearth of information on submissions and staff at the printed magazine. For a magazine extolling the virtues of on-line-ness, this lack of on-line contact information seems peculiar.

Targeted

The periodicals that furnish you with the most visitors may not be those devoted to the Web. As long as your site has fairly specific subject matter, and magazines and journals exist that target the subject, you have a great Web-independent opportunity to develop hits.

Don't let the brevity of this section fool you. Magazines and journals targeted to your audience can be the source of a server-jamming quantity of visits. Each individual site will need to approach its own targeted periodicals, so I will simply give you some general tips; you must then go out and develop your own pool of sources.

Your home brewing site may be ho-hum for the editors of *Internet World*, but the editor of *American Brewing* might be interested in giving some space to a review—which will be read by exactly the audience you want to reach. Trade magazines, in particular, can be a great source of visits, because they are often on the hunt for material. If your industry or field doesn't yet have too many participants with their own Web sites, trade magazines may be overjoyed to feature you in an article, column, or editorial. For these magazines you should probably contact editors or columnists directly and try to establish a personal rapport. At the least, send them a press release.

In that same vein, specialty magazines and journals can provide a great return on investment for your advertising dollar. The relatively low cost of the ad and the appropriateness of the audience make a combination that's often impossible to beat. Be sure to run your telephone number in small ads, because some people still exist who will wonder what that funny www. thing is. (For a discussion of on-line advertising, see Chapters 8 through 10.)

Books and CDs

As with magazines, there are now countless heavy Web-related tomes (often packaged with CDs) available, each claiming to be the definitive directory of Web sites. With some, you merely have to send the author your URL in order to be included. But be careful: many of these books don't want to hear from you, instead they depend on their own contributors or editors to find and review sites. I list here some of the more prominent book/CD combinations that accept submissions; some of these have reached classic status and are updated regularly, while others are part of the ever-increasing crowd of newcomers that spring up from month to month. So consider checking the bookstore periodically to see if a new, submission-friendly volume has come out.

New Riders' Official World Wide Web Yellow Pages

New Riders' Official World Wide Web Yellow Pages (aka *NROWWWYP*) represents the annual print and CD version of the popular Web site `http://www.mcp.com/nrp/wwwyp`. The book is as thick as its name is long and is considered one of the great authorities on Web site listings. Like a telephone yellow pages, *NROWWWYP* organizes its information by subjects that include just about everything. Even so, most buyers probably employ the book as a door stop and rely on the CD, which provides hotlinks to Web sites when you click on a listing's URL.

To submit your site to *NROWWWYP*, go to `http://www.mcp.com/nrp/wwwyp/submit.html` and fill out the form. You will be included in the online version for sure and probably included in the print and CD version, although the editors don't guarantee it.

Que's Mega Web Directory

And mega it is. *Que's Mega Web Directory* yearly directory lists over 18,000 sites on over 1,000 pages. The information is also listed on the accompanying CD in a searchable form that features hotlinks to the Web. The book and CD are alphabetically organized by topic. Although the book contains numerous design aids to help navigate and highlight information, most users will just plug in the CD and click away. You can submit your URL for inclusion in the next version to either Dean J. Rositano or Robert A. Rositano at `info@simply.com`.

Walking the World Wide Web

Walking the World Wide Web includes over 750 pages, most of them listings of Web sites. This periodically updated directory and guide doesn't go for the comprehensive approach but rather tries to separate the wheat from the chaff by providing an extensive review of each site listed. Author Shannon T. Settle's Web-savvy approach helps the reader surf the Web efficiently and productively. Walking the World Wide Web also includes a CD with the requisite hyperlinks to Web sites. To submit your site, go to `http://www.vmedia.com/vvc/`

onlcomp/wwww2nd/recommend.html and fill out the form. Or you might send the information directly to author Shannon T. Settle at shannon@vmedia.com.

Your Business

Most businesses—and for the purpose of this discussion, your Web site is considered a business—generate a tremendous amount of material, most of it on paper, directed to other businesses and to the general public. These various bits of printed material, whether they are business cards, stationery, press releases, brochures, catalogs, or advertisements, represent an opportunity to get your URL in front of someone. In addition, you can mention your URL in on-line letters, lectures, interviews, and presentations, building a visitor base from the ground up. Don't miss *any* opportunity to get your URL out to the public.

Printed Materials

One only has to glance at a newspaper or a magazine to see the rapid proliferation of URLs in advertisements. Whether or not you choose to go the paid advertising route, you can promote your URL in printed matter right at hand. Your URL should be as prominent as your phone number on business stationery and business cards. Marketing material such as press releases, brochures, and catalogs should include your URL near your address and phone number.

Make sure that your site caters to the readers of any of these media whom you wish to draw in. For example, if you include your URL in a brochure, at the very least include information relating to the brochure on your site. Better yet, give the brochure customer a little something extra at your Web site. For example, Lands' End, the clothing catalog, has a special Internet store at their site http://www.landsend.com that features specials and closeouts for the Web customer.

Sigs

Sigs, the automatic signatures you can set up with many e-mail programs, can be a great source of promotion for your URL, especially if you design your sig in a way to stand out from the crowd and reflect well on your site. Sigs have been part of the on-line world since the early days of e-mail, so there isn't a design that hasn't been tried nor a quote that hasn't been included at one time or another.

Make sure your sig is clear and includes plenty of white space, and that it makes your best pitch to attract people to your site. Keep it short; any more than eight lines will stretch most readers' patience to the breaking point. Be wary of complex graphics (for example, reproducing the Mona Lisa using slashes and asterisks). To promote your site, consider mentioning prominent awards or including a line from a positive review. You'll definitely want to let people know what they can expect from the site and to highlight the site's unusual allure that will spur them to visit.

Don't try to do too much with a sig. To preserve precious space, consider leaving out your e-mail address (the receiver should already have it in the header of your message). You may want to design a number of sigs and use them for different occasions, including a default sig to highlight your site and standby sigs to promote other aspects of your business. Use the standby for communications that don't involve your site, such as messages to competitors. Figure 7-1 shows a sig with about everything wrong.

```
----------z a p . c o m----------
How Your Computer Can Hurt You -- And What You Can Do About It
1619 Eighth Avenue North, Seattle WA 98109 (206)2837636
don@zap.com / donsellers@aol.com      http://www.zap.com

            Q <==\
  W <=====----|  \
 E<======          \--------
  R<======                        OUCH!!! What do I do now?
   T<===== -------------
    WHY?

Fax: 206.285-0308
------------------------------------------------------------
```

Figure 7-1 An extremely busy sig.

Figure 7-2 shows a distillation of the same material, in a compact, easy to read form.

Everything Else

Not a day goes by when you won't have an opportunity to get your URL into the mind of a potential site visitor. If you give a talk or lecture, consider putting your URL on slides, overheads, or handouts. If you are interviewed for print,

```
========================================
 ZAP!              http://www.zap.com
 A Resource on Computer Related Injury
 Don Sellers, Director  (206) 283-7636
 1619 Eighth Ave. N., Seattle, WA 98109
========================================
```

Figure 7-2 Same sig, different sentiment.

television, or radio, be sure to mention your URL at least once. Lucy Mohl, the brains behind film.com, gave a short interview to a radio station in Australia that had a Web site. Noting her URL, they put a link from their site to hers; now she gets 300 visits a month just from that one site. That's not enough to make a site viable in and of itself, but, when added to the other opportunities presented in this book, it can be significant.

Don't overlook the possibility of including your URLs in some inexpensive advertising. In the documentary film industry (in which I work in during my spare time), it is customary to send postcards announcing when a documentary will be broadcast. The shiny side of the postcard usually carries a photograph from the doc, and salient information is printed in the message section on the card's reverse side. Postcards like these can be used as an inexpensive vehicle for advertising Web sites as well. They can be targeted to a select audience and don't need to contain much copy, since your site will furnish the content.

8

ADVERTISING OVERVIEW

The primary goal of Web advertising is to draw visitors to your Web site, where you present your content or further advertising messages in a controlled environment. Success is usually measured by how many visitors you draw and how many ultimately buy your product, but that's not the only measure. Many Fortune 500 companies use their million-dollar Web ad budgets just to generate brand and company awareness. Companies such as Saturn want their customers to know that this car manufacturer resonates with the new generation and can communicate with them using the new medium.

Attractive design and stimulating content will draw a crowd to your site, but if you're offering high-budget excitement and magic to potential visitors, you may find that directory and search engine listings don't draw enough of an audience to pay the bills. If this is the case, the best way to increase attendance at site is to advertise, usually on the Web itself—usually with a banner ad (see Figure 8-1). The same goes for small Web sites. You can easily promote your smaller site with a banner ad at least as attractive as a Fortune 500 site; the only difference is that you might choose to buy fewer impressions or to advertise with a smaller, less-expensive provider.

In previous chapters, you've seen how to draw visitors to your site using directories, search engines, discussion groups, and other promotional tools. Once you've produced an ample number of links and referrals to your site, you will

Figure 8-1 A typical banner ad.

quickly discover whether the traffic generated satisfies your business objective. If not, it's worth the time to investigate whether to launch a Web advertising campaign. There are thousands of Web sites that sell advertising space, and rates run from under $100 per month to the tens of thousands. What's right for you? Without committing a lot of money or resources, any Web site can test a Web advertising campaign in order to determine the viability of a full-scale effort.

Internet evolution has been so dramatic that it has inspired a new paradigm for time measurement. An "Internet Year" is equal to 2.5 months. By this measure, you may get the value of one to two years of experience with your business model within your first six months of Web advertising. So buckle your seat belt for the faced-paced roller coaster ride of Web advertising.

In this chapter I introduce the history and basics of Web advertising by discussing a host of different Web ad campaigns. In the subsequent chapters I dive into the nitty gritty of how to get the most out of you Web ad buck.

Brief History of Web Advertising

The history of Web advertising is a chronicle of how the Web's dynamic growth took shape based on the need for Web businesses to stand out in an ever rising sea of on-line congestion. It's also the story of how the on-line advertising form itself has evolved as technology has improved and competition has grown.

Beginning of Commerce on the Internet

The World Wide Web services of the Internet were first made available to the public in 1993. Commercial restrictions on the Internet were lifted in the winter of that year, enabling Dale Dougherty to launch the first magazine-like commercial publication on the Web, GNN (now owned by America Online). The beta version of the first graphical browser, Mosaic, had been released in April 1993, giving the then-two million Web users a way to view the full text and graphic content of GNN and other early Web advertising sites such as Mercury Center, Hotwired, and Internet Shopping Network. These sites attracted the first on-line advertisers such as Microsoft and MCI.

These pioneers had an established model for how to host and price advertising and sponsorships: the commercial on-line services including Prodigy, CompuServe, and America Online. By 1993, these services, running independently from the Internet, had already been operating on a commercial basis and had millions of subscribers. It was here that the first banner advertising, scrolling banners, and sponsored content promotions were used. Interactive advertising agencies such as Modem Media were founded to make use of and expand upon these on-line advertising forms, in anticipation of business demand for professional advertising campaigns.

By early 1994, commercial sites were springing up on the Web at a growth rate greater than 20% per month. The Web still provided an uncluttered forum for large national sponsors such as Mastercard and American Airlines; however, the primary advertisers during this era were vendors of technical products and services. At the same time, small businesses that couldn't afford the rates for banner advertising or couldn't find a commercial site with a suitable audience began to experiment with alternatives.

In 1994, Canter and Siegel tried to bring direct advertising to the Internet (see "Spamming" in Chapter 6, *Mining the Hidden Gold in Mailing Lists and Newsgroups*). Although flogged by many in the on-line community, Canter and Siegel's message appealed to others and netted them over $100,000 in business. More important, their notoriety led to a greater awareness that the Internet had become a commercial entity. The walls of the "free forever" Internet culture soon came down.

Early Advertising Strategies

In 1994, Yahoo and a dozen other Web directories and search engines were launched. By entering a keyword or subject, Web users could find your commercial Web site almost as easily as they could find a shop using the Yellow Pages. This enabled the commercial sites—notably on-line vendors of computer and technology products, specialty products such as wine and flowers, and services such as travel—to grow exponentially using little more than the free directory listings. As sales grew, so did demand, and it became necessary to continue investing in one's new Web business.

These early sites were thus compelled to supplement the directory and search engine listings with formal advertising campaigns. The on-line magazines provided a natural forum for business advertising, and the magazines in turn found the need to launch their own ad campaigns in order to reach a subscriber base that could support competitive ad rates.

Web ad rates were initially structured like those of specialty print magazines in the $20–$80 CPM (cost per thousand impressions) range. Led by major sites such as Yahoo, Netscape, and CMP TechWebRates, rates have generally trended downward since, although they are still comparatively high if measured based on return on investment.

Not Free Anymore

Web commerce was well established by the end of 1994, and some of the first success stories were being acknowledged in the press by way of vehicles such as the Tenagra Awards for Internet Marketing `http://www.tenagra.com`. One of the first Tenagra awards went to Pizza Hut, who launched a Web ad campaign to send visitors to its storefront on the Web; while not directly selling many pizzas, the campaign did manage to generate positive publicity and increase brand awareness. The Internet Shopping Network, later bought out by Home Shopping Network, proved that consumers would visit an Internet "mall" and actually buy goods and services in meaningful numbers. Finally, a software game developer, id Software, used Web advertising to widely distribute a free sampler of DOOM, which became one of the best-selling computer games of all time.

Between Netscape, which distributed millions of free beta copies of Netscape Navigator to anybody who would click on their banner ads, and the software companies like id Software, the "free" culture of the early Internet was successfully supplanted by commercial enterprise. When the free teasers initially offered by companies were phased out, Web users realized that they actually had to pay for products and services, and only then did they begin to understand that the Web was no longer an ad hoc philanthropic organization.

New Advertising Directions

By 1995, it became apparent that a business had to establish a Web site presence on the Internet to be considered a "modern" company. Instead of directly promoting their wares, businesses would advertise on the Web in the hopes that visitors would click on the banner ad and hyperlink to the businesses' actual Web site. Here the business could make their sales pitch in earnest to qualified buyers. This structure developed because the typical banner ad, at about three inches by one inch with a short message and simple graphics, simply couldn't provide enough information. And so Web advertising and Web site promotion became a sort of package deal. However, savvy Web visitors quickly grew wary of and bored with this approach to conveying an advertising message, since it basically amounted to simply dressing up a traditional sales pitch in snappy electronic clothing. So Web advertisers began to experiment with new types of ads, some of which continue to this day. Examples of the most important new approaches that were developed during this period (1994–95) follow in the sections below.

Fun Content

Some early Web ad agencies, including Modem Media and Organic Online, downplayed the sales pitch in their advertisements and lured Web visitors to the sponsor's site with fun content. Their campaigns for sponsors such as Zima attempted to build ongoing relationships with customers and to give the customers new reasons to visit the sponsor's site. For their campaign, Zima `http://www.zima.com` ran hip banner ads on popular Web sites. The ads drew Generation X visitors to the Zima alcoholic beverage site, where themes like favorite TV shows and dating spurred repeat visits and interactive participation. The ads now draw about 40,000 visitors monthly; however, Zima acknowledges the only way to gauge success (that is, increased sales) will be by conducting surveys.

Fictional Characters

MCI followed up a heavy TV advertising blitz with banner advertising for their "Gramercy Press" Web site `http://www.mci.com/gramercy/`, a fictional publishing house with a cast of office characters. This campaign yielded over one million hits from 14 countries, and the fictional receptionist, Darlene, received 150 e-mail fan messages per week—including marriage proposals! Visitors to the site bought thousands of MCI software packages at $99 each, one of the first instances of money actually changing hands for products offered on the Web.

Global Reach

Mastercard `http://www.mastercard.com` positioned themselves as a global corporate citizen by using banner ads designed to appeal to an international audience. They chose international cultural themes such as folk tales and flags from around the world offered visitors additional folk information for various countries via a simple click on the banner ad. Embedded in the entertaining content was information on Mastercard offices and cash machine locations around the world. The ad campaign now attracts thousands of visitors daily from Europe to Australia, and the company has been successfully acquainting their customers with the idea of making financial transactions over the Web.

Lifestyle

For its Web campaign, Toyota advertised heavily with new model introductions and contests. They established a site designed first to appeal to the lifestyle of active young adults, and only second to provide product information. Toyota's site highlighted career and cultural articles that contained no automobile sales message and attracted repeat visits and, as a result, repeat advertising impressions. One benefit of this approach was that the repeat visits didn't require an additional banner advertising investment, since the visitors would "bookmark" the Web address and return on their own. Of course, there's still no guarantee that they'll buy a new Toyota.

Impact of New Technology

During 1995, true, interactive multimedia technology arrived on the Web—encouraged and supported in large part by Netscape. In response to Web clutter, more ads featured animation, audio, and even full-motion video. 1995 saw other on-line developments as well. The first on-line radio station, Radio HK `http://www.radiohk.com`, was launched by one of the first Web ad agencies, Hajjar/Kaufman. Hotwired persevered as the first on-line magazine exclusively supported by advertising—even as it lost money. Time-Warner Pathfinder, ZD Net, and other Web spin-offs of successful print publications were launched, gained huge audiences almost overnight, and quickly became the advertising sites of choice on the Web. However, while they do sell a good deal of advertising space, they are essentially funded by their successful print counterparts.

Another familiar name, Ragu, was named to the 1995 Tenagra awards list. Like the technology vendors, Ragu had a qualified target audience on the Web—any of the six million users who enjoy good food. But where any food vendor can develop a fun and informative Web site, Ragu took interactivity a step further with sweepstakes promotions, with prizes including a fully paid trip for the entire family to Italy. Ragu was able to use these ads effectively in drawing consumers to their site to enter the contest; from the information on their entry forms, these respondents also provided Ragu with valuable demographic information. So in addition to building brand awareness, Ragu managed to build a detailed profile of visitors who were open to providing this information as part of a contest entry.

Java, Active X, and other new Web technologies were the highlights of 1996. These new technologies led to the development of metascreens, webcasting, targeted banner ad rotation, and other banner ad formats more similar to television commercials than to static billboard ads. Web traffic audit systems such as I/Pro and PC Meter were recognized for their utility in verifying the Web audience for advertisers. Security concerns became the single biggest obstacle to conducting commerce over the Internet, which led to the development of countless electronic commerce technologies.

Toward the Future

When, if ever, will Hotwired and other original-content, ad-supported sites turn a profit? It's difficult to say. Even the popular Yahoo Web directory, with one million visitors per day, can't yet survive on advertising alone—although they have sold enough to provide the means to recently float an Initial Public Offering. Even so, it is rumored that 80% of available advertising inventory on Yahoo regularly goes unsold. The viability of the popular advertising sites is becoming an important issue for the Web advertisers who depend on them.

According to Jupiter Communications `http://www.jup.com` and SIMBA Information Inc. `http://www.simbanet.com`, advertisers spent about $45 million on the Web in 1995. It's hard to imagine such a huge medium surviving much longer on such a (relative) drop in the bucket. But these same studies predict that ad spending could reach $2–$5 billion by the year 2000, while other studies arrive at projections of $80–$120 million in ad spending for 1996 and $700 million–$1.4 billion by 1998. That's quite a future!

Advertising Vehicles

Most Web advertising relies on the ubiquitous banner, but new types of advertising opportunities are being introduced every week. Here's a breakdown on the composition and use of banners, followed by a rundown of other options for advertising on the Web.

Banner Basics

Banner advertising is typically sold by the impression, also called a "Page View" or an "Exposure." An impression simply means that a visitor to a Web site viewed a page containing your banner ad. It doesn't mean they saw or read your ad, and it doesn't mean they clicked on it. It simply means that they were exposed to it—it's up to you to make sure to catch their attention so they will look at it.

Overall, on average, you can expect that 2% to 3.5% of visitors who see your ad will actually click on it in order to visit your Web site. Ideally, you would only pay for those who click through to your site. A small number of Web sites charge based on click-throughs, but this is not a popular pricing method, because it penalizes the advertising site itself if your ad is poorly designed.

Web ad sites typically charge a set rate for anywhere from 50,000 to 5 million impressions. Small ad sites generally charge a monthly rate without necessarily guaranteeing the number of impressions you will get. There are many sales pitches used to try to divert your attention from this issue, but if the site is unwilling to guarantee a minimum number of impressions, you are probably paying too much. The same is true if they will only give you a figure for hits: a hit, at best, means that the visitor was exposed to some page on the Web site, possibly one at which your ad was not even displayed.

The typical banner ad has a rectangular shape and measures approximately three inches across by one inch deep. Advertisers must deal with extreme size and image quality limitations for their banner ad since the standard .GIF graphic format allows only 256 colors and around 72 dpi resolution. This standard exists as a concession to the relatively slow performance capabilities of the typical modem, as well as to the speed limitations of the Internet in transmitting files. It's remarkable that banner ads with graphics, photo images, and animation look as good as they do. They are, however, very convenient and economical, since they can be easily created by anyone with a personal computer and some graphics software.

Where the Banner Waves

Your choices for where and how to plan your banner ad are virtually limitless. Some sites offer special benefits you should bear in mind.

Search Engines and Directories

Popular spots for Web banner advertising are the directories and search engines, since they reach a large audience and can provide highly targeted advertising delivery for an extra cost. You can expect to pay $25–$40 CPM to purchase the minimum number of impressions, typically 100,000; the more popular search engines such as Yahoo usually are at the higher end of the range. The search engine route is usually the first choice for Web sites that can afford $2,500–$4,000 per month on advertising—about the same rate you might pay for a page in a small circulation trade magazine. If you are ready to commit to volumes of 500,000 impressions per month or more, you can expect to pay around $20–$25 CPM, a big savings.

For this investment, you can typically specify that your ad should only display for a targeted category such as arts, education, or business. You can expect to pay double if you want to target a highly-specific category such as "dry cleaners." Since a directory such as Yahoo receives one million visitors per day, they will rotate your ad with others so that each advertiser gets its turn and is guaranteed the impressions it has purchased. You will pay less for a longer-term commitment, but initially you may be better off committing to a month or less in order to determine if this type of banner advertising will pay off for you.

Another search engine advertising option is available: the purchase of keywords. The folks at the search engine companies figured that if they not only sold banner advertising and contest promotions but also charged to have your banner ad display only when a keyword such as "widget" is searched, everyone would benefit. Instead of the $20–$40 CPM typical for a standard banner placement with search engines, you can count on a $40–$80 CPM if you buy keywords. You can see how popular this form of Web advertising has become by testing a search engine with a popular keyword such as "car" and seeing how often an ad for a car-related business is displayed (see Figure 8-2).

High-Traffic Content Sites

The second choices for banner advertising are popular news sites such as CNN and USA Today and popular technology sites such as Netscape. You can expect to pay about $20–$30 CPM, more if you want to target a very specific audience.

Another type of high traffic content site exists. These are sites designed to reach some very specific audience. There are sites to attract game enthusiasts (Happy Puppy), stock investors (Quote.com), entertainment buffs (Mr. Showbiz), automobile shoppers (Dealer Net), computer enthusiasts (ZD Net, c|net), food lovers (Epicurious Magazine), and so on. You can expect to pay $30–$80 CPM to advertise on these popular sites.

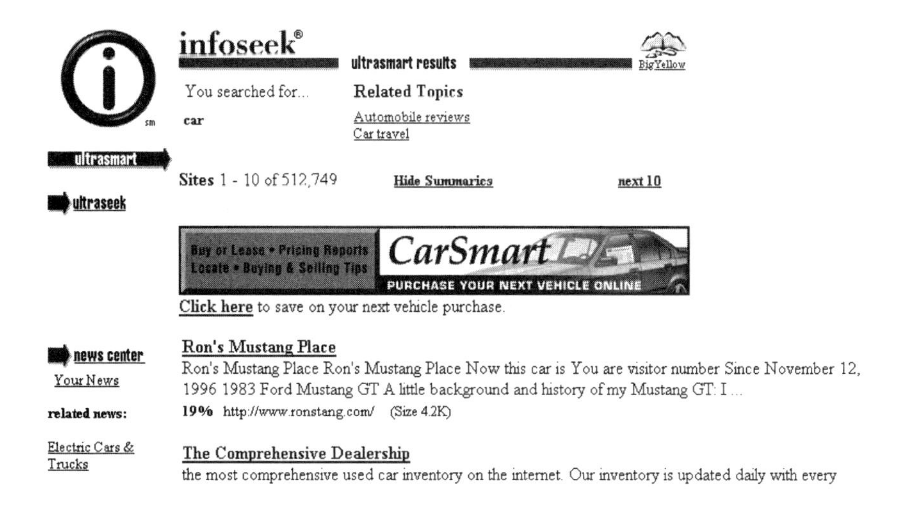

Figure 8-2 Result of a search for "car" in InfoSeek.

Small Targeted Content Sites

You might expect that smaller Web sites would offer better advertising rates. Unfortunately, this is not the case. Since they can only sell you 10,000 to 100,000 impressions, smaller sites must charge more in order to make their service viable. You can expect to pay $30–$80 CPM for small targeted content sites, which are geared towards an industry such as real estate or an interest group such as tennis enthusiasts. Good buys are rare, but they are available; these will be explored in Chapter 9, *Launching Your Web Ad Campaign*.

Contests/Sweepstakes

Contest and sweepstakes promotions are usually presented as banner advertising, but they will cost at least twice as much and generate many times the click-through rate of the typical banner ad. Since an easy contest entry for a car or trip is appealing to many Web site visitors, the click-through rates can be phenomenal—as can the opportunity to obtain user demographics on the entry form. Yoyodyne `http://www.yoyo.com` attracts game players with free games and contests, which are subsidized by sponsors. The tremendous response rate to contests enables the company to guarantee click-through visitors at a rate of 50 cents per click-through, which is substantially less than the $1–$2 average click-through cost. But since the visitor is only clicking on your ad to enter a contest, the true value of this approach is hard to determine; furthermore, as in the case of Yoyodyne, the benefit clearly goes to Web sites that cater to software game players. Figure 8-3 shows a typical Web sweepstakes promotion.

Metascreens

I have a simple definition for a metascreen: a banner ad, typically animated, that appears full-screen for 5 to 30 seconds before the Web site content is displayed. Buying a metascreen is one way to assure that your ad won't be missed. For example, Duracell `http://www.duracell.com` used a metascreen ad to have a Duracell battery "burst through" some popular Web sites such as Yahoo and GNN. By clicking on the battery, the whole page would rotate, revealing Duracell batteries behind the page itself. Of course, forcing people to view advertising is risky, because it could result in users refusing to return to a site. At this stage, metascreens remain an experimental buy for those who have a large budget.

Want to win a Nissan Pathfinder? It's as easy as 1-2-3!

Step 1: Click to go to any of these participating websites.
(The numbers in parentheses tell you how many sign-up pages -- and chances to win -- are at each site):

Greater Pacific Trading Company (3)
Hollywood Online (3)
NetGuide Live (5)
NetRadio (3)
Thunder & Lightning Company (3)
Yoyodyne (1)

Figure 8-3 Automobile sweepstakes sponsored by NetGuide.

Finding Help

If you can't decide where to advertise, you can let an advertising broker such as Double Click or Narrowcast Media select a group of Web sites for you. These sites represent, or broker, the advertising space for anywhere from 15 to 1,000 Web advertising sites. The rates can vary from $30–$60 CPM depending on how specific an audience you wish to target. The sales pitches of these brokers can be very compelling: some will guarantee a 20% click-through rate, compared to the industry average of 2%. Others will make sure your banner ad displays only when a visitor to one of the sites in your package deal matches specific criteria such as sex, profession, computing platform, hobbies and interests, or all of the above, which costs a lot more. The buying power of ad brokers leads to economies of scale and allows the brokers to deliver more select visitors rather than random repeat visitors by selecting the right mix for you.

Testing Your Banner Ad

You will be able to determine almost immediately if your banner advertising is successful, by seeing how many visitors click through to your Web site. The ISP who hosts your Web site usually provides you with a raw traffic log that indicates how many people per day visited your site and which pages they visited. The numbers should jump dramatically after your banner ad starts to run. If they don't, you might want to redesign your banner ad, which the advertising sites allow; this is explored further in Chapter 9. *Launching Your Web Ad Campaign.*

If you want to test the waters, you can join a link exchange, a free reciprocal banner advertising exchange program. Thousands of other Web sites will take turns displaying your advertising banner, and all that is required of you is to allow a single, rotating banner ad on your site. The advantage—other than the free advertising—is that you will get reports showing how many people clicked through on your banner ad. If you don't like the numbers, you can experiment as often as you wish with new, fine-tuned banner ads.

New Opportunities

The technological advances that Web advertisers will be able to take advantage of in the future are being introduced now. At the same time, old technologies are being used in new ways. Here's a smattering of the new opportunities for advertising on the Web.

Audio Ad Delivery

Real-Audio and other software developers distribute free software in order to make sure that Web users can listen to audio content over their computer speakers. Radio stations have taken advantage of this, and national networks such as ABC and NPR now "broadcast" radio programs over the Web. This may be an excellent vehicle for advertisers who have found success on the radio; you can expect to pay $35 CPM or more for a 15–30 second audio message.

Real-Time Audio and Video

Just as with audio, Shockwave, Java, Vivo, and other free programs are now available to Web users so they can view audio-video clips on their computer. Some of the newer technologies allow smooth, real-time delivery of these clips, and new Web sites are starting up, such as First-TV, to take advantage of the technology both for content and for advertising. For $70–$85 CPM, you can run an audio-video commercial on a popular computer site such as c|net or on a search engine such as WebCrawler. For example, Sony chose WebCrawler for a new personal game machine product introduction. However, at this point, this vehicle is more for capturing attention than for cost-effective advertising for the typical business.

Webcasting

Many companies are using the Web as their distribution vehicle for news and information services. In order to compete with CNN, USA Today, and other top news sources, these news delivery services, known as webcasters, distribute free e-mail accounts (Gold Mail, Juno) or free screen savers (Pointcast Network, Freeloader). You subscribe to the delivery service by providing some basic demographic information, and in return, the service delivers free e-mail or news services that contain animated banner ads. The Pointcast Network `http://www.pointcast.com` boasts over 1 million customers who view news feeds from Reuters combined with animated advertising throughout the day. Advertisers pay around $3 CPM for their ad but must purchase 20 million impressions. What they get is an ad that is seen by the same audience, day in and day out, for the entire month. Pointcast is extremely successful and is usually sold out of advertising inventory, indicating that it is a popular and successful buy for companies that can afford it. Microsoft is entering the Webcasting scene, and this competition may adversely affect Pointcast and the others.

Custom Sponsored Editorial Content

Web sites such as Homearts Lifestyle, which is the master site for Redbook, Good Housekeeping, Country Living, and other popular magazines, work with advertisers to build exclusive brand-building marketing programs that integrate advertising material into editorial content. The best example is recipe columns that include recipes that in turn require ingredients from a popular food manufacturer. Polaroid sponsors a section of Parent Soup, a Web site for parents, that tells parents how to improve their kids' self-esteem with instant photos. The potential advertising power of custom editorial content is countered only by the potential for a negative response to mixing advertising with editorial.

Sponsored Chat Rooms

These are similar to sponsored content sites in that they directly identify the advertiser as the sponsor. Inquiry.com, a personal dating search service, sponsored a banner ad on the Webgenesis `http://www.Webgenesis.com` Singles Chat Room—a very clever tie-in. K-Swiss, the shoe manufacturer, pays Webgenesis based on click-throughs to their sponsored chat room, Club K-Swiss.

Sponsored Content

Interactive fictional story lines and soap operas are developing a substantial following, and many sites will be happy to place your product into the story line for a fee. For example, the New And Kewl site `http://www.new-kewl.com` offers a product placement example, buried deep within an interactive story episode: "... And with that stood up, slipped a mitten-like protector over each ear, and stormed out into the cold evening, leaving Cave alone with his glass of Old Crow ..." (see Figure 8-1).

I know guys who have been at Whitbred Industries
for years and they hate him - they say he sat on
their proposals, or that he took their constructs
and never gave them their due for their
accomplishments. But they'll never leave. It's an
obsession: you have to make Thomas Whitbred give
you respect."

CAVE
"These guys at the corporation - who are they? Give
me some name."

FINK
"Oh, no. I'm no snitch. And, anyway, I'm
not fired. I have to go call Mr. Whitbred."

And with that stood up, slipped a mitten-like
protector over each ear, and stormed out into the
cold evening, leaving Cave alone with his glass of
Old Crow.

-- back --

Figure 8-4 A link in an interactive story.

When you click on the hyperlink "mitten-like protector" you are taken to a Web site which sells Earz brand ear-muffs (see Figure 8-5). This type of interweaving of product placement, which is obvious (a hyperlink) yet non-intrusive (you can choose not to click on the hyperlink) is very clever and can yield a fun surprise. I believe that sponsored content could be around for a while, and that on a site such as New and Kewl, it has the potential to attract visitors who are hungry for information and eager to explore.

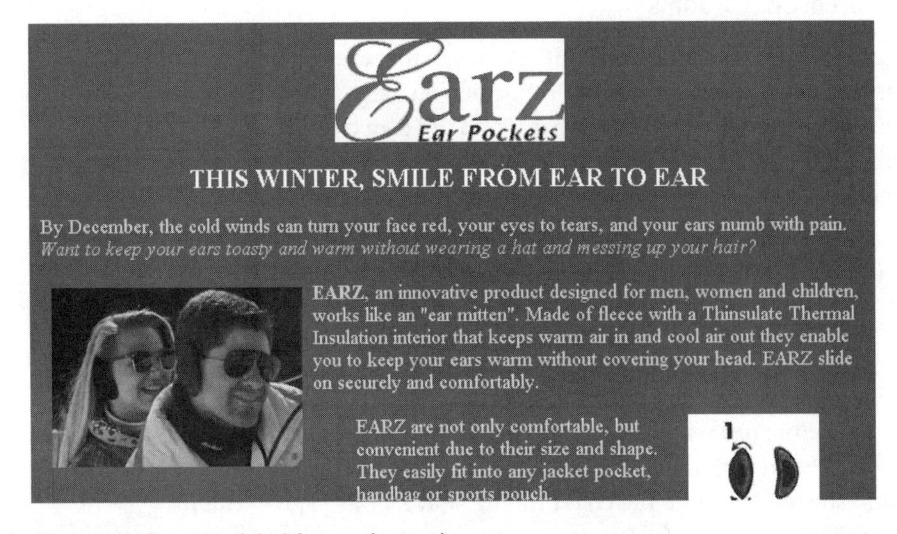

Figure 8-5 Sales site linked from an interactive story.

Local Sites

Before the Internet explosion, small businesses typically chose newspaper advertising to reach local customers. These same newspapers are now on the Web, and they are discovering exciting advertising opportunities for small Web sites catering to a local or regional business clientele. In one example, Papa Joe's Pizza in Houston has successfully used cybercoupons, which they sponsor through the *Houston Chronicle*'s Web site. Companies such as Multi-Ad Services Inc. `http://www.multi-ad.com` will give you the scoop on hundreds of manufacturers such as Sony who are willing to divert co-op advertising dollars to reimburse local Sony dealers for Web advertising. Other newspaper sites will help you sponsor on-line contests and promotions geared to your customers. These newspaper sites need your business, and they will work hard to help make your investment pay off.

Who Is Advertising Online

In a 1995 fourth quarter study from Webtrack `http://www.Webtrack.com` the 15 leading Web advertisers in dollar volume were names. The list appears to represent a "Who's Who" of corporate America—with a few surprising exceptions.

AT&T led the pack, with $567,000 spent. Netscape was a close second, with $556,000. The Internet Shopping Network came in third, at $329,000, followed by a host of well-known companies like NEC, Mastercard, American Airlines, and Microsoft. However, surprises were to be found in the tenth spot: Sportsline, an on-line sports news subscription service; and in the fourteenth: Music Boulevard, an on-line music store.

According to another study, in the fourth quarter of 1995, 176 sites were actively advertising and 102 sites were successfully selling ad space in measurable amounts. Even with a rate of growth of 20% per month in these figures, there is still tremendous opportunity to advertise your Web site and leap out through the clutter, making an impression ahead of your competition.

What does the top 15 list have to teach us about advertising on the Web? First, it indicates that even the largest of the Fortune 500 companies such as AT&T are spending only a tiny fraction of their eight- and nine-figure advertising budgets on the Web. For these established companies, Web advertising primarily serves the purpose of building brand loyalty rather than generating actual sales returns. The big companies are, for the most part, using the petty cash drawer for experimentation, yet at the same time they have found an inexpensive way to position themselves on the cutting edge, at the forefront of the new global village.

Note some of the exceptions—the companies that are themselves Web creations, such as Internet Shopping Network, Sportsline, and Music Boulevard. The very existence of these companies depends on Web business, and as a result the amounts they spend on Web advertising make up the largest percentage of their advertising budgets. The very fact that they are listed in the Top 15 indicates a confidence in Web advertising and commitment to the success of their sites for the long term—even if profits don't flow right away.

Ad Bargains

It can't be emphasized enough that all Web advertisers are building for the future, since even the most successful ones—such as Virtual Vineyards, with $1 million in annual revenue—need to continue growing just to recoup their investment in software development and other start-up expenses. Do you really have the time, the money, and the patience to commit to such a project? Would you be willing to operate on a smaller scale?

If your answer to the second question is yes, there is good news. As you will see in Chapter 10, *Refining Your Web Ad Campaign*, there are many Web advertising bargains to be found. One of the best is a package of 10,000 impressions for $295 dollars offered by MMGCO `http://www.mmgco.com`. But you'll have to decide whether the 200 visitors (or 100, or 400, depending on the targeting and quality of your message) who will be attracted to your site will spend enough to justify the investment.

A Sophisticated Buy

In Chapter 9, *Launching Your Web Ad Campaign*, I will critically examine Web advertising rates. Just to get your juices running, here's an example of a good buy. Targeted advertising to buyers of music run $40–$100 CPM. That $40 turns out to be a very good deal for companies like Music Boulevard `http://www.musicboulevard.com`, which can go to HotBot and buy their ad offering that is targeted to .edu domains. These domains are primarily college students, who are one of the single largest markets for music.

Let's say Music Boulevard purchases a three-month ad for $195,000. Using the low end of the rate scale, $40 CPM, simple math lets us arrive at a projection of 4,875,000 impressions. For simplicity, let's use the overall average Web ad click-through rate of 2%, even though Music Boulevard undoubtedly will do better because of their well-targeted audience. This gives us 97,500 visitors (2% of 4,875,000) to the Music Boulevard Web site for the three-month period. This means on average that each visitor must purchase $2 worth of merchandise just to cover advertising costs. I presume that Music Boulevard will do better than this.

Now that you have a basic idea of whether you are a "player" at the low end or the high end of the Web advertising pyramid, it's time to launch your campaign, which we will explore in the following chapter.

9

Launching Your Web Ad Campaign

Department store founder John Wanamaker once said, "I know half of my advertising is wasted. The trouble is, I don't know which half." Advertising experts would claim that it doesn't matter, as long as enough of your advertising hits its mark.

The planning of a Web advertising campaign often becomes a time for much soul-searching about your site. When you begin to consider paying for the opportunity of attracting visitors, you start to realize you must be crystal clear about your site design, who you want to draw to it, what advertising message you will use to lure them, and where you might place this message to reach the greatest number of potential visitors. Then you need to design a number of different banners and prepare to test and test them again to see which ones in which types of placements produce the most click-throughs to your site.

Get It Right

Anyone who has rushed to meet deadlines on the production and submission of advertising material for print or television might find the production cycle of Web advertising to be a bit of a luxury. After all, even after your banner ad has been submitted to a Web site and displayed on pages, you can change it frequently and easily according to your own schedule and needs. Additionally, you have the benefit of receiving real-time results in the form of concise reports drawn from traffic logs. If you do make a mistake in your message or design, you can correct it before all of your impressions are "spent." With the technology and resources available to create and modify banner ads and to monitor the results, you have an excellent chance of getting it right with Web advertising.

As stated previously, getting it right requires the right audience, message, content, and ad placement.

Defining Your Target Audience

Who is the typical prospect for your product or service? If you have already been marketing it successfully, you should have a very good idea of the types of people or businesses that are prime targets for your Web advertising message. If your business is new, use the search engines to find businesses of a similar nature, and try to determine who they are targeting their message to.

In any case, use whatever information you obtain to develop a profile of your target audience. This should be broken down by ranges and/or percentages for the following categories: age, sex, education, location, income, interests, occupation, company, purchase authority, and any other categories you consider appropriate. This will give you a shopping list to use when you are selecting sites to advertise on, since many sites can provide you with a good profile of their target audience. However, keep in mind that it is not just a matter of finding the closest match; rather, what you are seeking is the best balance between what you can afford to pay and what the site charges for delivering a close, closer, and closest match of your target audience.

You can match your laundry list of target audience demographics to the list provided by many Web sites, such as Hotwired. Although research indicates that 60–70% of Web users are male, sites that offer content and value for women can attract just as many qualified buyers as sites which do the same for men. A good example is the success of the Homearts Lifestyle site. Again, although Web users are overwhelmingly white, the same goes for minorities. Net Noir, with content for black Americans, and new sites targeted for Asian Americans are increasingly attracting active visitors open to targeted advertising messages.

40–40–20 Rule

A common rule in direct mail is that the quality of the mailing list contributes 40% to the results of the mailing. The content of the mailing—that is, the nature of the product, the service, and the price—constitutes another 40%. The final 20% is the presentation of the message. The same issues are relevant with Web advertising. The quality of the demographics available to you from the Web site should contribute 40% to the results of your ad, and so on.

Targeting Broad Demographics

New software is emerging that enables a Web site to help you target the right audience for your ad, even if the site's own audience is not very well defined. This software reads the domain of the visitor to help determine who they are and where they came from. On sites such as HotBot, you can pay to have your ad displayed only when visitors with your selected targeted domains visit the site. This enables you to target employees of a specific company, such as ibm.com; visitors from a selected country, such as .uk for United Kingdom; college students, from .edu domain sites; and much more.

Refining Your Message

Refining your message in order to meet the interests of your target audience may require you to revise the content of your Web site as well as the message content of your ad. According to Arial Poler, chairman and founder of Internet Profiles Corporation, "The real ad is the Web site itself." It is important to the success of your campaign that you understand the relationship between the banner ad and the Web site.

Banner Ad=Envelope; Site=Message

You need to attract qualified, interested buyers to your site where they can see what you have to offer. Search directories will deliver visitors who have invited themselves, but in order to sustain a business effort, additional traffic must be drawn to the site. According to Roy Schwedelson, CEO of WebConnect, "The banner is like the outer envelope of a direct mail piece, and the Web site compares to what is in the envelope." The banner ad serves as an invitation designed to capture the attention of your target audience, who then must open the invitation to view the message.

Boosting Message Effectiveness

Many methods exist for increasing the odds that a large number of people will find your invitation irresistible to open and read. For some sites, the value of word of mouth promotional efforts such as contests, giveaways, public relations efforts, and Usenet discussions significantly boost the impact of the advertising message. (For more on Usenet, see Chapter 6, *Mining the Hidden Gold in Mailing Lists and Newsgroups.*) In addition, the "cachet factor"—earning a reputation as a site of superior interest—substantially affects the impact of an advertising message, as popular "Internet only" companies such as Virtual Vineyards and Amazon.com have discovered. Personalized customer service, valuable content, and a commitment to quality can all add a cachet factor that attaches to your advertising message over time. On the other hand, some companies, such as the Vermont Teddy Bear Company, have discovered that the cachet factor they enjoyed in direct mail did not transfer to the Web. Therefore, it's best to assume, no matter how popular and well liked your businesses is, that you start from ground zero on the Web.

Designing Banners That Work

Your banner ad is a very small piece of Web page real estate. There is little room for telling your story; you have little time to capture the attention of the Web user. However, if designed well, even simple ads can offer sizzle without distraction and without requiring an effort on the part of your reader.

Remember AIDA

AIDA (get Attention, arouse Interest, stimulate Desire, ask for Action) is the standard technique used to draw people to read and respond to a direct mail promotional offer (see "Achieving AIDA," sidebar). The rules are the same for a banner ad. The design of your ad along with a few keywords should be used to get a seeker's attention and to arouse their interest. Additional words about benefits, shown in a smaller text size, should be used to stimulate desire.

Extensive testing of various banner ads suggests that getting a viewer's interest is not enough. You cannot assume that prospects will know that a click on your banner ad will produce a payoff. Your ad has to accomplish a final task, a call to action—it must get them to click on the banner and visit your Web site. This is often done by using a small button or box within the banner that reads "Click Here." Tests have shown that the simple addition of the "Click Here" is a call to action that can double or even quadruple your click-through rate. For an extra call to action, you could insert clickable text below the banner "Click Here for Special Offer." Adding urgency, such as a limited-time offer, helps stimulate action.

ACHIEVING AIDA

You can achieve AIDA in many ways:

Product Information—Touting features and benefits

Social Role and Image Information—How to impress others

Hedonic Pleasure—Providing amusement or entertainment

Public Causes—Environment, education, health research, and so forth

Economic Benefit—How to improve your living standards

Intellectual Curiosity—Material of inherent interest

Tony Hsieh of Link Exchange knows banners: Link Exchange's reciprocal banner program generates millions of banner ads per month. The research they have put into their own ads proves that a call to action can significantly increase hits for a thoughtfully designed ad with useful information. Others agree: The design should be attractive and not overpowering, and the text must have content that triggers clicks. CyberAtlas reports that adding information to ads can increase click-through rates by as much as 20%.

Click-Through Caution

Free offers, contests, and sweepstakes are an effective way to increase the click-through visitation to your site. However, if you go this route you will only get not only qualified prospects, but many unqualified prospects who are looking for a freebie. Thus, the best way to improve click-through is perhaps the worst way to improve sales to qualified buyers. Worse yet, you will use up your impressions on people who don't meet your target audience. One exception: if your product is an impulse buy, then a free offer can be just the ticket.

Adjusting Message and Color

Internet Link Exchange experimented with phrasing such as "100's of sites with Links Back To Yours—Free," "Get Your Web Page Linked To The World," "Do you want more HITS for only $0?", and "More hits for FREE—Click Here." The last phrase was 58% more effective in getting click-throughs than the first phrase (see Figure 9-1).

Once Link Exchange settled on the most effective banner, they experimented with color combinations for the "Click Here" button; they found that the ideal

Figure 9-1 Link Exchange's experimental phrases.

color combination was 26% more effective than the worst color combination. These results hold up over tens of thousands of impressions and are statistically significant. To say that blue works better than red or yellow would oversimplify the process, but, to give one example, it appears that a solid color border around the ad helps imply that the whole banner is clickable. You should also keep in mind that some of your visitors will be viewing your ad on a top-quality computer monitor displaying in 800 by 600 dpi, while others will have a low-quality VGA monitor in 640 by 480. You should test view your ads on a variety of computer monitors to make sure they can properly display your design. The point is that you should continue fine-tuning your ads and review the results carefully.

Be Early, Be Big

In designing your banner ad, keep in mind the layout of the Web page on which your ad will be displayed. The first screen, or the top of a Web page, is the first thing a site visitor sees. The highest click-through rates are for ads displayed on the first screen, since many visitors to the page will view only that screen and then click to another page, without scrolling all the way down to the bottom. Unfortunately, even if the visitor didn't see your ad at the bottom of the page, it still counted as an impression, since he or she was exposed to the page and had the opportunity to see your ad.

As you would expect, larger banners of 500 pixel width or more are clicked on more than smaller ones. Some Web sites allow a choice of sizes, but the majority don't. However, there is a trend towards a wider variety of shapes as well as sizes, and you may find it useful to design a different ad for every Web site you advertise on.

Some Effective Banner Ads

A good starting point for viewing simple banner ads and their click-through results is a visit to the White Palm Comparison Page of Link Exchange member banners `http://www.photolabels.com/clickthroughcomp.html`. This site provides on an ongoing analysis on what is working in banner advertising; here are some examples.

"Shrink your GIFs up to 90% with GIF Wizard." This banner ad (see Figure 9-2) yielded 4.4% click-through for a software product aimed at any Web site owner. The benefit is clearly defined in the text.

Figure 9-2 A GIF Wizard Banner Ad.

"Real Estate Agents—Increase your Sales with PhotoLabels—Click Here." This ad (see Figure 9-3) appeared on a random group of Web sites not necessarily targeted to real estate agents. Yet this company knew that the ad, which included a sample graphic of the PhotoLabel, could capture the attention of any agents passing through. The ad yielded a 3.9% click-through.

Figure 9-3 PhotoLabel's Real Estate Agent Ad.

"Warning—Do Not Play Blood 3D If You Have Nightmares ...." Created for a computer game, this ad (see Figure 9-4) capitalized on consumer curiosity, yielding a 2.6% click-through across a broad range of untargeted Web sites.

Figure 9-4 The Blood 3D Banner Ad.

Placing Ads

Web advertising gives you more options for ad placement than more traditional advertising forms. You have the flexibility of selecting one or many sites to advertise on, and you can choose to place ads yourself or to use an advertising network or on-line agency.

The minimum criteria for choosing a Web site on which wants to place your ad should be a guarantee of about 10,000 visitors per month. Rates should be based on CPM, and your decision to advertise should be based on site demographics or visitor value.

Becoming proficient in placing ads means finding good ad value, knowing how to buy keywords in search engines, working effectively with advertising reps, or perhaps doing the whole job yourself. Finally, you may be able to run a successful advertising campaign without laying out a dime—you can instead barter for ad space.

Finding Good Value

The Web is a great place to find advertising bargains. The field is still new, and competition is growing. With traditional forms of advertising, bargains are available, but generally only to ad agencies and large companies who can guarantee large purchases over time. In contrast, many Web sites—even those with published rates—will consider your offer, even if it is very low.

To find good advertising values, you must first know the ins and outs of rate cards. Then look for the bargains, and don't expect to find them all in the basement; sometimes the swankier, more expensive sites can deliver the best return on you advertising investment.

Know Your Rate Cards

A rate card is a document that should provide all the information you need on ad rates, banner ad size, submission specifications, contract issues, company background, and visitor demographics. Some rate cards exist as pages on the Web site, while others are available on request. Many sites now publish ad rates and related information on hundreds of other sites. For example, Webtrack `http://www.Webtrack.com` offers rates and demographic information for over 800 categorized sites of all sizes, while SI Software `http://www.sisoftware.com` is a resource site that offers a list of over 400 links to sites that publish ad rates, advice, and other information.

The rate card should include information on the number of hits, subscribers, and visitors, as well as available advertising inventory. Some will tell you how many pages the average visitor reads and how much time they spend at the site. Rates should be quoted in CPM or click-through. Even though CPM, or cost per thousand impressions, is a very imprecise tool for measuring value, it's the only one that can be consistently applied to any Web site. Traffic counts for a Web site will tend to underestimate visitors and impressions. This is because many Web browsers and commercial services will "cache," or store frequently accessed pages and display them from memory rather than actually revisiting the Web site.

Any volume discounts and advertising agency discounts that are offered should be mentioned on the rate card. The availability of tracking and audit reports, frequency of banner rotation, and other high-tech capabilities are listed. Any available visitor demographics such as age, sex, gender, occupation, income, interests, modem speed, company type, size of company, and purchase authority should be provided. The rate card should indicate when the site was first launched, what awards have been received, and a background on the company that owns the Web site. It should clearly define what the goals and purpose of the Web site are, and it should also clearly lay out what the Web site will do for you to make your advertising campaign successful.

Unfortunately, most rate cards do not provide this kind of detail. You will find rate cards that quote rates that appear to have no correlation to CPM, and other that include no information on demographics, even though a demographic compilation is as simple as including a "Guest Book" form on the Web site.

Levels of Values

While it would be ideal to view advertising bargains by target audience, it's not practical, considering the tens of thousands of distinct products and services that each have their own ideal target audience. It's easiest to view advertising bargains by similar groupings of CPM, then identify what is a good deal in that range. Refer to Table 9-1 to see how advertising sites compare in cost versus category.

TABLE 9-1 VARIOUS ADVERTISING OPPORTUNITIES

CPM	Search Engine Targeted	Search Engine and Keywords	High Traffic Sites	Small Targeted Content Sites	Contests and Sweepstakes	Metascreens	Audio Video	Sponsored Content or Editorial	Special
$5					Pointcast				
$15				Homescout, Consummate Winsock App's					
$20	Yahoo		Pathfinder, Netscape						
$25		Open Text							
$30	Excite–Targeted City		USA Today, Quote.com	Internet-Sales Newsletter					Webstep $295 Trial Buy
$35	Lycos–Targeted Company		Mr. Showbiz						
$40+	HotBot–Targeted Domain.EDU		Dealernet Auto, Internet Movie DB						
$50–60			Advertising Networks						
$60–65			Technology Magazines, NBA.com					Homearts Lifestyle	
$70+						Webcrawler			
$85					Yoyodyne		c|net		
$50/click									

Table 9-1 Various advertising opportunities.

Bargain Basement

Ad rates and offerings change frequently. For example, you can pay as little as $3 CPM—an incredible bargain rate—for animated banner ads on the Pointcast Network, a Webcasting site; but you will have to buy a minimum of 20 million impressions.

At the next level up is the rare bargain found at small targeted content sites (see Chapter 4, *How to Get Quality Links*). These sites specialize in a profession such as real estate or an interest such as tennis. While most such sites will charge prices in the $30–$80 CPM range, you can find occasional offers around $15 CPM if you look hard. Sites offering a discount rate include Homescout, a real estate database Web site that delivers homebuyers with high-quality demographics, and Consummate Winsock App's, a software listing and review site. Besides the low cost, another benefit of the bargains in this category is the potential for higher-than-average click-through rates due to the quality of the target audience.

The next spending level is around $20 CPM; there are many good bargains in this range, including the Yahoo and Open Text directories, Time-Warner Pathfinder news site, Netscape's Destinations package, and ESPNET Sportzone. Most of these deals require a purchase of several hundred thousand impressions per month for several months; the sites are not highly targeted.

Mid-Level Bargains

$25 CPM will buy low-cost targeting in specialty newsletters, delivered via daily e-mail to subscribers. These newsletters, such as the Internet-Sales Discussion Group, are not cluttered with advertising messages and reach a very proactive Web audience. (For more about mailing lists, see Chapter 6, *Mining the Hidden Gold in Mailing Lists and Newsgroups*).

The publisher of the Internet-Sales List, MMGCO `http://www.mmgco.com` will help you test your banner ad by placing it on five selected sites for $29 CPM for 10,000 impressions. This gives you the benefit of very low cost entry to the banner advertising scene and enables you to test and fine-tune your ad until you get the results you seek.

For $30 CPM, you can find many good general as well as highly targeted ad buys. You can target a region or city on the Excite search engine or a general rotation on USA Today. For just a little more, around $35 CPM, you can target a specific country or company on Lycos. For $40 CPM, you can target a specific domain, such as .edu, with HotBot—perfect for reaching college students.

Bargains at the Top

Advertising networks represent, or broker, the ad space for 15 to 1,000 sites (see "Working with Advertising Representatives," below). For $30–$55 CPM, advertising networks will place your highly-targeted message on a combination of sites that they consider most suitable. Their knowledge of the market, buying power, and ability to help you maximize the reach and targeting of your ad can be very useful. One of the selling points of the networks is that they can negotiate bargain rates more effectively for the sites they represent.

The on-line PC magazines from ZD Net, c|net, CMP TechWeb, and IDG Publications are some of the most successful sites at selling advertising space. You can expect to pay $40–$75 CPM to sell your high-tech products here. Entertainment, finance, automotive, and food sites will run anywhere from $30–$80 CPM. There are not many bargains to be found in these higher-traffic categories; the best you can do is compare rates for similar sites, and observe which ones are more popular with advertisers. If a comparable site is more expensive but more popular with advertisers, there may be a good reason for it.

For $65 CPM, you can run a Metascreen, which functions like an animated, full-screen television commercial, on sites such as Homearts Lifestyle. You are guaranteed to capture the attention of Web visitors, though perhaps at the expense of some good will. C|net will sell you a multimedia banner ad that supports Real-Audio, Java, and Shockwave audio and video technologies for $85 CPM. Finally, sponsored game sites such as Yoyodyne offer free interactive games to visitors, which are subsidized by sponsors who offer free prizes. You can buy advertising for 50 cents per click-through.

Buying Keywords

Buying keywords on the directories and search engines is a powerful tool for targeting your banner ad to appropriate sites. When you buy advertising with the directories, you can pay extra to have your ad displayed only when specified keywords are searched. A good example of a potentially effective keyword campaign would be the purchase of the keywords "headache," "pain," and "arthritis" for a maker of pain relievers. You will usually double the cost of directory advertising by purchasing keywords, but there are some good deals available, such as $25 CPM with Open Text and Starting Point.

Cathay Pacific Airways began their Web advertising campaign in August of 1995 on InfoSeek. Today more than half of their registered visitors are referred by their InfoSeek banner ads, which read "Win 1,000,000 Miles." They bought several keywords, including "vacation," "tour," "airline," "weather," and "contest."

The only time their ad appears is when somebody uses InfoSeek to search for one of these keywords. This promotional offer has produced a 3.2% click-through and over 100,000 "CyberTraveler" enrollments, with 500 to 1,000 more signing up daily. The airline's goal was less than half this amount. The airline has tracked travel bookings by site visitors, and, in one year, several thousand of the registered visitors have traveled to Asia using Cathay Pacific. While there is no way of knowing how many of these purchases were based on the Web ad campaign, company officials noticed that many of the bookings came from places where Cathay Pacific has never used traditional advertising.

Of course, success is a matter of perspective: the airline has not generated significant new revenue, despite investing $150,000 in building and promoting the site. But the airline did accomplish their primary goal: to economically reach a 50-state market. And they have continued the campaign with an increased budget.

Working with Advertising Representatives

There are two types of advertising representatives: on-line advertising agencies and advertising networks. They both sell advertising on sites, but they do so in different ways.

You can find a list of links to advertising agencies that specialize in Web advertising at Admarket `http://www.admarket.com/Agencies/service.html`, or by using Yahoo or the other directories and search engines. These agencies make money in several ways: designing Web sites, assembling marketing information to develop ad campaigns, designing the ads, and placing the ads with Web sites. At every step, you can expect a 15–30% markup on their costs for commissions and fees; you might be billed by hour or by month. In return, you gain a single, knowledgeable source to handle all of your advertising needs.

Advertising networks work a bit differently from agencies. Rather than handling your campaign and Web site development from beginning to end, the networks represent a select group of Web sites and are usually the exclusive representative for them. They will help you find the right mix of Web sites for your target audience, but only from among the sites they represent. An advantage they offer is expertise in assessing the demographic profile of the sites they represent. Another advantage is that they may be able to spread your message to a larger portion of your target audience than would a single-site ad placement, which reaches the same audience over and over again.

Do It Yourself

Web advertising agencies may become commonplace in the future; but, for now, many businesses know that they can do it themselves and put their money to other uses. The main reason for this is the nature of a banner ad. You can easily create an ad on your personal computer in an hour or two, where a print ad or television commercial requires a tremendous production effort involving dozens of talented professionals. What's more, many rate cards will provide a complete set of instructions for how to order, pay for, and submit your own ad.

When negotiating for rates, remember two things. First, you may be quoted a high "gross" rate, that is, the rate they will charge you to place the ad directly, as opposed to the "net" rate charged to advertising agencies—which is often substantially lower. However, the second thing to remember is this: you can often achieve a price much lower than the rate card, if you ask for it. You can, for example, propose a trial run as a way for a site to "rationalize" accepting a lower rate. However, keep in mind that some popular sites, such as Yahoo, function more like traditional advertisers who won't veer from the rate card.

As the advertiser, you must become familiar with the advertising contract. Web advertising contracts will specify rates, impressions, guarantees, duration, ad position, rotation terms, terms and conditions of payment, the dates and time when your banner ad file must be received by the Web site, and when it can be rotated. As a new advertiser, you can expect a full credit check or a requirement for advance payment, at least in the beginning. Later the terms are typically Net 30 (payment due within 30 days of services rendered). If your campaign is not working and you choose to pull out, you may be obligated to pay the full amount of the contract or a smaller penalty to terminate. Regarding duration, Web advertising contracts are similar to print contracts: the longer the contract, the lower the rates you can get. But a longer contract can also lock you into a deal that might be bettered by something else next month, so it's advisable to limit the duration of your contracts until you have a very good idea of what works.

Barter May Be Better

You may be able to barter for ad space in exchange for cash and/or reciprocal ad space on your site. This is best illustrated by the relationship between the search engines and Netscape. Each engine pays about $2.5 million in cash and $2.5 million in barter to Netscape for favorable mention on their Netsearch page and for favorable positioning.

There are several banner ad reciprocal exchanges, such as the Link Exchange `http://www.linkexchange.com`, that rotate your banner ad among a thousand sites for free in exchange for your hosting another site's free banner ad on your site. You will also get real-time traffic statistics, which will show you very quickly whether your ads are effective. This is clearly one of the best deals on the Web, as the exchanges will let you change your ad every two or three days until it's perfect. However, keep in mind that the number of impressions you will receive on other sites under this arrangement is entirely dependent on the level of traffic on your site. If you have a high-traffic site, you will be rewarded with a high level of ad placements on the other participating sites. If your site is new, it's unlikely that you will get enough impressions to make this a true advertising alternative.

10

Refining Your Web Ad Campaign

The ability to easily refine a web ad campaign makes it unique among advertising forms. Many traditional advertisers have discovered the hard way that when any link in the advertising chain breaks, there is no ad campaign, let alone opportunities for campaign refinements. The broken link could be as simple as a model who arrives late for a camera shoot or a scratch in a film. Many links can break when a minor mistake snowballs through many stages before being discovered. The bills will come anyway.

Most traditional campaigns don't reach the stage where the chain can't be fixed, but the tax in personal time and effort to resolve problems is a high price to pay in order to implement the originally planned campaign on schedule and under budget. Web advertising frees you from most of these time and budget constraints, as well as from most people problems. It may free you from many of the equipment problems, too.

You can easily adjust your Web advertising campaign by scrutinizing reports, then testing and refining your campaign to maximize return on investment. Your goal is to have a site that will draw repeat visits, which means you must maintain and update the campaign constantly.

Reports

Real-time demographic reports exist in traditional media, primarily in television. Nielsen families and focus groups with response meters in hand have provided large national television advertisers with real-time reports for many years. But advertisers in other mediums have been left out. Their reports are usually based on the number of reply cards, amount of walk-in traffic, or number of phone calls received from an ad. The disadvantage of this is that the report results can't be assessed until after the ad campaign is over and the money is spent.

Web advertising generates numbers—more numbers than you will probably need. They can reside on your Web site, on the Web advertising site, or on the site of an audit bureau, commercial statistics provider, or advertising network. There are software programs available, such as StatBot, designed to compile and present the raw data from any one of these sites into extremely useful charts and diagrams (see Figures 10-1, 10-2, 10-3, 10-4, and 10-5). Two reports in particular will be of value to you: the one available from your site and the one from the Web advertising site. The report generated from your site will indicate the amount of traffic and will give you a general idea of who is visiting you and where they are coming from. The report from the advertising site will show you

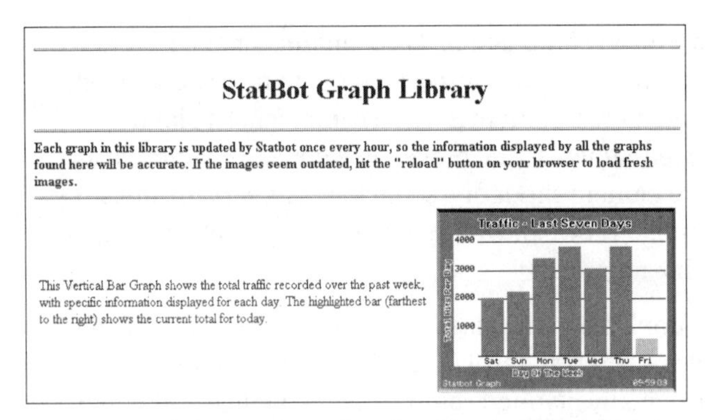

Figure 10-1 A StatBot chart of total traffic over last week.

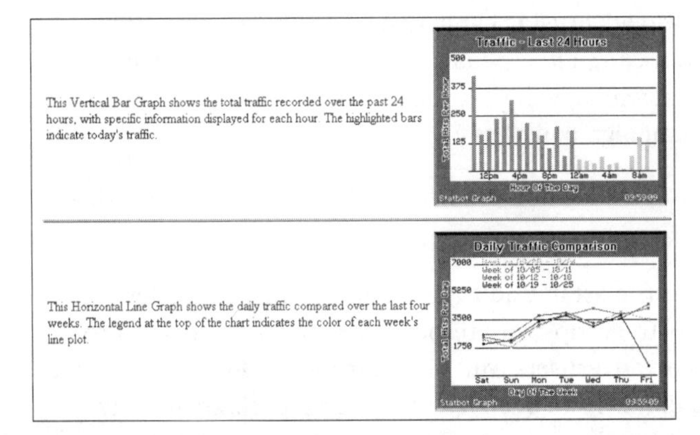

Figure 10-2 A StatBot chart of daily traffic.

how many of your impressions have been used and on which pages, with perhaps some additional demographic information. The reports provided by analysis services such as I/Pro `http://www.ipro.com/` will use additional information provided by the visitor's Web browser to offer you a concise view of who your actual target audience is.

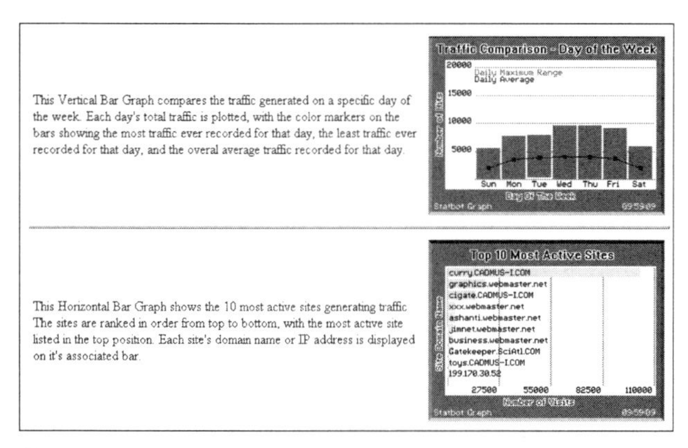

Figure 10-3 A StatBot chart of the day of the week and active site.

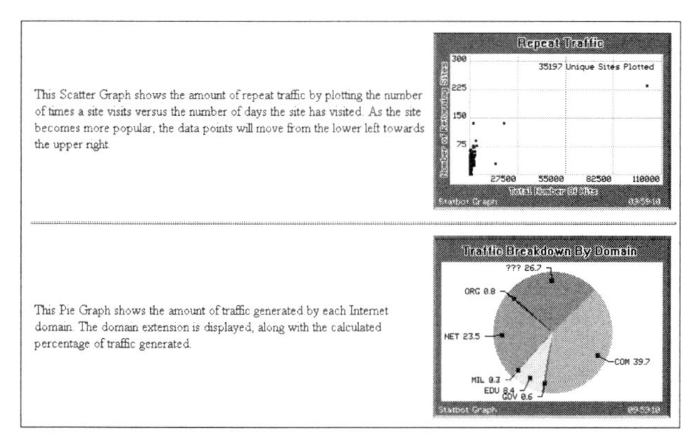

Figure 10-4 A StatBot chart of Repeat traffic and traffic domain.

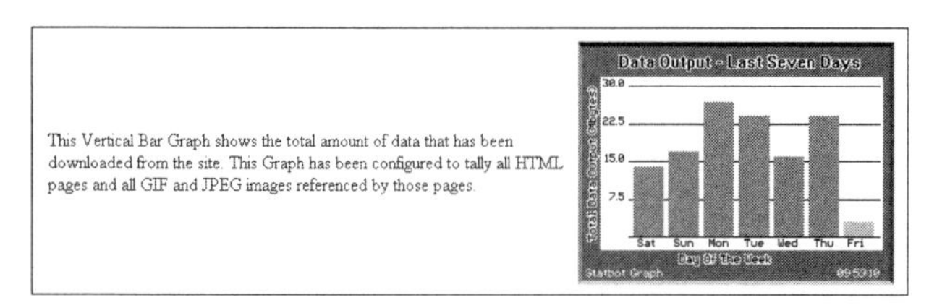

Figure 10-5 A StatBot chart of Total amount of download.

What Do These Numbers Mean?

The Common Log Format (CLF) is the standard for most of the Web servers on which your Web site might reside. CLF exists as a text file in the log directory of the Web site. It logs a separate record for each hit and can be parsed in a lot of different ways, both simple (asking it to count the number of times "aol" appears over a day or week) or complex (feeding it through an analysis program). You will probably have access to an ongoing, daily log report as well as a very large, cumulative log. It will report the following information on every visitor and what activity they had on your site: host/ip, RFC name, logname, datestamp, retrieval, code, and bytes. (Note that many servers offer an Extended CLF, in which the previous page [referrer URL], browser name [user agent], and cookie [persistent token] are also recorded.)

```
jdoe.cns.hp.com - - [24/Oct/1996:05:45:40 -
0400] "GET /sirate2.htm HTTP/1.0" 200 9860

jdoe.cns.hp.com - - [24/Oct/1996:05:45:41 -
0400] "GET /internet.gif HTTP/1.0" 200 10475

ppp25.hil.tele.dk - - [24/Oct/1996:08:24:44 -
0400] "GET /internet.gif HTTP/1.0" 200 10475

ppp25.hil.tele.dk - - [24/Oct/1996:08:24:44 -
0400] "GET /new.gif HTTP/1.0" 200 1322

ppp25.hil.tele.dk - - [24/Oct/1996:08:25:05 -
0400] "GET /silink2.htm HTTP/1.0" 200 24576

38.228.234.102 - - [24/Oct/1996:08:46:53 -
0400] "HEAD / HTTP/1.0" 200 -

pm1_110.pionet.net - - [24/Oct/1996:00:13:43
-0400] "GET /new.gif HTTP/1.0" 200 1322

pm1_110.pionet.net - - [24/Oct/1996:00:13:46
-0400] "GET /internet.gif HTTP/1.0" 200 10475

pm1_110.pionet.net - - [24/Oct/1996:00:13:59
-0400] "GET /silink2.htm HTTP/1.0" 200 32768

s56.salc.wsu.edu - - [24/Oct/1996:00:52:11 -
0400] "GET /new.gif HTTP/1.0" 200 1322

s56.salc.wsu.edu - - [24/Oct/1996:00:52:11 -
0400] "GET /internet.gif HTTP/1.0" 200 10475

s56.salc.wsu.edu - - [24/Oct/1996:00:52:46 -
0400] "GET /silink2.htm HTTP/1.0" 200 109260
```

Host/IP

The first field in the record is the host/IP. It indicates the hostname of the visitor or an IP number if domain name server lookup is not enabled for that visitor. The example above shows many types of host/IP visitors. The first is readily identifiable by the company of origin, hp.com. The next visitor, with the .dk extension, is from Denmark. The third visitor was reported by their IP number because their system does not support reverse domain name lookup. The fourth visitor is a customer of a .net (usually an ISP). The final visitor appears to be student from a readily identifiable university, thus the .edu domain extension.

RFC Name

The RFC Name is the remote identity or login identity for the user provided by the remote server. This log does not have RFC enabled, so the report returns a single dash: "-". Most sites disabled remote identity lookups in 1993 and 1994, as security concerns were raised.

Log name

If your site uses local authentication and registration, the log name will appear in the next field. This site requires no user id, therefore the field returns a dash: "-".

Datestamp

The next field is the datestamp, which is useful when running the log figures through analysis software. The datestamp information can be used to graph peak activity throughout the day, week, and month. This will show you whether traffic picked up after your banner ad started appearing.

Retrieval

The retrieval method is posted following the datestamp. In the examples above, GET/silink2.htm indicates that the silink2.htm file was retrieved by the visitor. The visitor with the .edu extension retrieved three files that make up a single Web page. You may see POST and HEAD in the logs as well. POST indicates that the user sent data, usually when filling out a form and clicking the submit button. HEAD indicates a browser or caching server just checking to see if the file has been updated since the last time it was retrieved by the checking machine.

Code

A 200 code indicates the retrieval was successful. Many other codes are used to indicate different statuses, such as the familiar 404, which indicates that a file was not found.

Bytes

This indicates the size of the file retrieved. This is important because many ISPs use bytes to measure the traffic activity that determines how much they will charge a Web site.

Optional Information

Even if you're only logging the above information, you can still identify patterns in visitors, traffic, and site usage. Commercial software can detect and analyze some of the information. It ranges in price from the hundreds to the thousands of dollars. Some run concurrent with the Web server and live on the same machine; however, more typical are post-log analyzers that can run under UNIX, Macintosh, or Windows (depending on the product) and import and analyze the logs at some point after the fact.

A second form of optional information can be bought from commercial statistics providers such as I/Pro. These services cost thousands of dollars monthly —although prices were substantially reduced in mid 1996—and require hourly or more frequent transmittal of your log to their remote site. They use their proprietary analysis software to provide you with a customized report that meets your exact needs. Advertising networks (see "Working with Advertising Representatives" in Chapter 9, *Launching Your Web Ad Campaign*) will usually offer enhanced information free of charge or included in the CPM price of the multiple-site buys they will place for you on the sites they represent.

Advantages of using the commercial services include their understanding of the numbers and their commitment to providing clean, audit-quality information. These services use sophisticated analysis and report software and hardware to crunch millions of records into a format that you can use. Depending on your budget, it might well be worth your time to look into what they offer, as number crunching at these levels requires time, computing power, and trained staff in any case.

A third source of information on the visitor may be found in data stored by the visitor's browser. Netscape Navigator and Internet Explorer, as well as several other browsers, support passing a token, called a "magic cookie" or just plain "cookie," back and forth between the browser and server software. These tokens can last for only a single visit to a Web site, or (with some limits) for years. Cookies are stored in a text file format on the user's machine, often in a cookies.txt file; you can open any word processor and take a look at your own cookies.txt file. Often this information comprises details you provided during registration at a Web site; other times, the server may simply pass a code that it uses to look you up on your return.

There's been a lot of hysteria about cookies, but they can't be used to grab information unwillingly. They're more like a chit you hand a doorman to get back in the club, than like a VISA card or your driver's license. Cookies are sometimes used to just generate a unique code for each visitor, which allows for tracking by user over time and analysis of other patterns without caring about a specific individual's usage.

My cookies file includes unique visitor IDs that I/Pro and Interse have assigned to me. The file also includes unique login names and passwords for registered sites. These cookie tokens are reported only to the site that originally sent them. Netscape Navigator 3.0 and Internet Explorer 3.0 both give the user the choice of whether to accept cookies from other Web sites.

Tracking Visitors

A unique visit, or individual visit, is generally counted every time a user visits your site. The visitor's host/IP is then reported to the log. Most report mechanisms will count a new visit if the visitor doesn't return within a half an hour. As things stand now, every individual visit to a page displaying your banner ad is counted as an impression. It's a very common practice in the Web community to discuss the individual visitor count when the actual count was individual visits. Whether the difference in these numbers is material at the site on which you advertise has to be examined individually.

If the Web server feeds a unique and persistent cookie, like a session number that is never sent out twice, it's possible to get a decently accurate track of the number of unique browsers at unique locations that visit the site. Since most people are using the same browser at the same machine, this number corresponds fairly well to the number of unique users coming to a site. Some browsers don't track cookies (less than ten percent and shrinking at most sites), and some people refuse to accept cookies (also a small number), so it's not a total solution. But it does give you something that approximates the number of unique individuals. Since you can track sessions (individual visits) separately, you can see how many times people return over the course of a few hours, a day, a week, or other time periods, depending on the flexibility of the analysis software you're using or the service you subscribe to.

Confusing as it all sounds, the technology to determine accurate visit counts has actually improved greatly since the bad old days, when sites were limited to using host names and IPs to track visitors and users, and weren't able to gather useful information about patterns over time.

Click-Through Response Rates

First, a reminder of what a click-through response is. User behavior or slow Internet speed might cause a user to click on your ad but not follow through to visit your site. They can halt the process by hitting the stop button on their browser or through other means. But the click will be registered at the Web advertising site, adding to their total of impressions on your ad. Unfortunately, the only accurate count of users who actually click through to your site is found in your own logs.

Numerous large-scale studies have been undertaken to analyze averages for click-through response rates. I/Pro `http://www.ipro.com/` recently announced that the overall average click-through rate for the entire World Wide Web is about 2%. This number means that of all the Web crawlers who see your ad on a site, an average of 2% will actually click through to arrive at your site. Since this included click-through rates of more than 2% from foreign sites, the average for US sites is actually less than 2%. I/Pro concluded that foreign click-throughs are higher, perhaps, because of the newness and novelty of Web advertising in other countries.

A study from Doubleclick `http://www.doubleclick.com/` of the sites they represent indicated an average click-through of 3.5% the first time the ad is seen, which declines to 2%, then 1% the third time the same ad is displayed. A study by Cyberatlas `http://www.cyberatlas.com` reported click-through rates ranging from .4% to 2.8%. Internet Link Exchange `http://www.linkexchange.com` reported an average click-through rate of about 3% for their thousands of Web site members. The numbers jump to the 3%–8% range for free offers, contests, and sweepstakes (see "Click-Through Caution" in Chapter 9, *Launching Your Web Ad Campaign*). Some advertising networks claim they will design a multisite campaign for you that will guarantee 20% click-through. Reports of click-through numbers will always skew to the higher end of the range, since ineffective ads are quickly dropped in favor of refined ads, and it's likely that only the improved numbers show up in the reports.

Test and Refine

Nothing can really prepare you for the feeling you get shortly after your first banner ad appears. As you look at the early returns, you might feel disappointment, even panic. If you've run your 300 impressions and only have had four or five or six people visit your site, you might begin to wonder if you made the right decision in the first place to advertise on the Web. Once you gain your composure, you will realize that this is what testing is all about, and that the biggest and most successful companies in the world test and fine tune their ads regularly, then wait for the law of large numbers to work their magic.

Determining The Best Banner

Testing and refining your banner ads can be done only by exposing them to hundreds of visitors. Standard statistical sample size numbers of 300 impressions or more should be adequate to predict the overall success rate of any single banner for the target audience that is reached. You might find that the click-through rate is unacceptable but the ad is a good one, in which case you will have to improve the targeting instead of the banner. Deciding whether the 1%, 2%, or 3% click-through you receive is acceptable must be based on your overall goals for the Web site and the campaign.

The only way to determine if the first banner ad was adequate is to test other versions. Link Exchange, for example, tests numerous versions of the same message. When they have found the message that works best, they test numerous design renditions of that message to improve it further. You will want to do the same in order to determine the best banner or banners for your Web site.

The first thing you must decide is what process you will use for testing your ad. As I discussed in previous chapters, Web advertising sites will allow you to change your banner as frequently as once a week, and some will allow you to rotate different banners during the same time period. The free reciprocal link exchanges, by comparison, will allow you to change your banners every three days. So the best strategy is to prepare several banner ads and have them ready to be submitted to the Web advertising sites and exchanges. Test as many as you can as quickly as you can, as long as each gets an exposure of at least 300 or more impressions. This is not a hard and fast rule, however. If your campaign will ultimately be aimed at several hundred thousand impressions or more per month, then a test of 1,000 impressions might be slightly more accurate then a test of 300.

As you begin to employ the techniques used by successful companies to improve their click-throughs, you will begin to appreciate the real-time nature of Web advertising. If you committed an ad to a newspaper or magazine, you would have one shot at getting the attention of tens or hundreds of thousands of readers. But banner ad testing allows you to finalize the most effective ad before 99% of your impressions have been "spent." On the other hand, you will have to remember that the "freshness date" of a banner ad is only about two weeks, so even the best ad will have to be refined.

Where's the Best Return on Investment

The same banner ad can produce widely varying click-through results on different sites. Fallon McElligott Advertising reported that their banner ad for Ameritech yielded the same number of click-throughs on the Mercury Center news site, which charges $3,100 a month, as it received from the Time-Warner Pathfinder site, which charges $30,000 a month, even though the audience is much larger on Pathfinder. Both sites provide daily news, but the Mercury Center site bills itself as the number-one news source for Silicon Valley companies and their employees. This leads to the conclusion that audience make-up is at least equally, if not more, important than audience size.

Another advertiser who experienced varying degrees of click-through success was Ferndale, an entertainment site that features an interactive soap opera. Cyberatlas reported that the site attracted a click-through of only .7% from a WebCrawler ad, 1.1% from an InfoSeek ad, 1.5% from Mr. Showbiz, and 2.8% from the same ad on Hotwired. But Hotwired has a CPM that is three or more times the rate of WebCrawler or InfoSeek. Whether it's worth three times the CPM to get three times the click-throughs is determined by the overall goals for your site and your campaign. These returns illustrate the difference between general, untargeted advertising on a search engine and well targeted advertising on a site such as Hotwired, which is known to attract a young, hip, interactively oriented audience—just the ticket for an interactive soap opera.

Your ROI, or Return On Investment, can't always be measured in dollars; it might be measured in terms of growth of subscribers or registrations to your site, or it could be measured using traditional surveys of visitor attitudes towards your ad and your site. Deciding how to evaluate the best ROI for your site may come down to comparing how well your ads and your site do against the competition.

Sites To Come Back To

The time and money you spend on advertising should result in visitors who will come back to your site repeatedly. Part of an ongoing campaign means having a site that will encourage return visits in and of itself. You can help ensure this by remembering that people return to sites they find entertaining, informative, and dynamic.

Entertaining

Entertaining a visitor is easy to do with a site that is fun by nature, but what if your product or service isn't "fun"? Consider these examples: The Tide Clothes line site `http://www.tide.com` is "dedicated to keeping your clothes looking their best." The What's New section features ongoing "Spin and Win" contests and offers "The Stain Detective," a fun, colorful, interactive tool to help you solve your worst cleaning problems. How about an on-line company store that offers unique detergent dispensers and Tide Stock Car Race Team clothing items? Is this any way to sell a boring product? You bet it is.

NASCAR fans love nothing better than getting a pit pass and talking to mechanics and drivers and watching the goings on. After every race, the NASCAR site `http://www.nascar.com` interviews drivers about the race, and visitors are invited to the "garage," where they can read the comments next to the driver's picture (see Figure 10-6).

The TV Guide Online site `http://www.tvguide.com` is an attractive and informative version of the printed guide. This alone is probably enough to get substantial repeat visits, due to the changing nature of the information and arti cles. But TV Guide went a step further, offering a television discussion forum

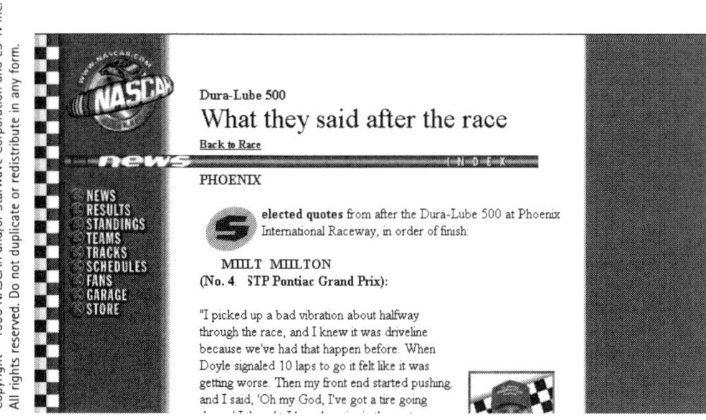

Figure 10-6 NASCAR's "garage" section.

and clips from very old *TV Guide* magazines, to remind us of what we were watching as children.

Informative

Many sites are being produced to resemble lifestyle or news magazines that almost completely hide the primary sales message. Numerous newsletters and news services exist that you can subscribe to and report on as effectively as the news sites; the targeted spin you put on the news will keep visitors coming back for more. For example, a wealth of public domain information from government and nonprofit organizations is available that is begging for a fresh presentation or a new spin. Many financially-oriented sites specialize in poring through volumes of government data in order to present only the most useful consumer information for their target audience. Intuit `http://www.intuit.com`, makers of Quicken financial software, are intent on introducing their customers to the benefits of doing financial transactions over the Web. In one section of their site, they have taken pages of raw data from the National Traffic and Highway Safety Administration and turned it into a colorful, informative, interactive page that tells drivers how safe their vehicles are. As these visitors dream about their next car, they keep coming back for more.

Informative sites also can be found that are lighter in message and tone. Advertising Age `http://www.adage.com` offers discussion forums on subjects such as ad campaigns, where people present some very strong feelings on what they like (such as Little Caesar's Pizza commercials) and what they don't (such as the Euro-pop teens in the Mento's mints commercials). Scott Donaton, the magazine's editor, keeps the discussion lively as a regular contributor and manages to offer fresh information not found elsewhere on the Web site. People keep coming back to see how the discussion threads play out.

The same goes for Chat rooms. Hotwired `http://www.hotwired.com` just launched a massive Chat room site to keep their subscribers who would otherwise stray to other Chat forums right at home. Visitors will come back to the site to get information from other visitors.

Dynamic

The Web enables and fosters change. In fact, the Web demands change. The technology that wowed your visitors last week may not impress them at all today. For a Web site to be successful, its presentation must be dynamic and must stand out from the crowd. One tool for achieving this is the new form of webcasting. Although the old Pointcast and Freeloader news and advertising delivery vehicles are terrific if you're a subscriber and are very effective for their advertisers, they don't deliver content from your site or from most others. However, newer companies like Surflogic `http://www.surflogic.com` now offer such updated delivery vehicles as the off-line browser—a sort of Web surf agent that works similarly to Freeloader, but with more user programming choices and no advertising. The new version enables Web site owners to distribute free software to their visitors that will enable these visitors to receive information from the site on a daily basis automatically. It's like offering all of the content and advertising of a Pointcast, except that you are the exclusive advertiser and content provider.

The power of webcasting is bound to increase. Netscape and Microsoft are currently in a bidding war to bundle offerings from top Web sites such as the New York Times and deliver the content daily to you via e-mail. Each company has lined up dozens of top Web sites and offers visitors free content that would otherwise require a subscription fee. As a way of maintaining brand loyalty, the service is only delivered to visitors who use one or the other browser. This free, daily e-mail distribution of Web content could take off to the point where smaller, more specialized sites might be invited to participate.

Continuing Campaign

Once you have taken all of the steps I have covered, you might feel like sitting back to enjoy a job well done. But the dynamic nature of marketing on the Web requires constant vigilance over your campaign and your site. There may not be much you can do to improve your product or service, but Web site visitors are a demanding lot, and they need new reasons to visit your site on a regular basis. In addition to the improvements in your content, you must constantly strive to develop and improve your ad campaign. It all goes back to the two-week "freshness" date of even the most successful ad; any ad will lose most of its effectiveness soon after the freshness date expires. This suggests that you may have to be constantly developing entirely new campaigns; in reality, you might only need a new way of posing and designing the same message. Or you might want to consider rotating the "persuaders" you use. If one feature or benefit worked, you might try a new combination of features or benefits. Once it becomes obvious that this approach is losing its effectiveness, it's probably time to consider a new type of persuader, such as a "curiosity teaser" or appeal to consumer need for financial security. Since you are able to test each banner over a small number of impressions, you have little to lose by trying out different messages to see which get the most attention.

Continuing the Campaign On Other Sites

The freshness of advertising on a particular site may wear out after enough of the audience has been exposed to your rotating ads (see "Click-Through Response Rates," earlier in this chapter). At that point, you are paying for frequency of exposure to the same visitors rather than reaching out to new ones. Before you arrive at this point, it will be time to develop strategies to reach new visitors within your target audience by moving your ads to other sites. You may find out that you had a good sense about why the new site was not your first choice—either it is more expensive, or it simply can't deliver the same numbers for you, even with your tested and proven ads. You will need to adjust your overall expectations for the ad campaign and your site over a longer time period—perhaps years of numerous campaign and site placement cycles. Eventually, you will want to find a balance between reach and frequency, cost and results, that gives you some stability over time. Otherwise, you will always be in the position of frantically searching for the next killer ad to make up for the inevitable dry spells.

Spot the Trends

The various reports available to you regarding traffic, sales, and other activities will quickly begin trending in one direction or another. In traditional forms of marketing, where the sales closing cycle is longer, the ability to accurately assess trends requires months of reports. On your Web site, the sales closing cycle is often much shorter. Combine this with the nature of the Internet time paradigm, where 2.5 calendar months is the equivalent to one Web year, and you should assume that changes in any of your numbers, even within a two week period, can be indicative of trends that require an immediate response.

Another way to follow trends is through daily readings of material at Web sites such as c|net `http://www.cnet.com`, Netguide `http://www.netguide.com/gen/page/Home`, Interactive Week `http://www.zdnet.com/intweek/Welcome.html`, and the other Web magazines dedicated to reporting trends on the Web. If new competition or useful technologies are being developed, you will find out about them here first. Many site owners find that the knowledge and experience of professionals who subscribe to the Internet-Sales Digest, the Internet-Advertising Digest, and other lists is invaluable as a breaking news source on tips and trends (see Chapter 11, *The Benefits of Professional Help*). You will also want to regularly visit the demographic and advertising network sites to spot early indicators of new trends. Finally, make a point of visiting any Internet conferences in your area. Sit in on relevant seminars, and visit the exhibitor areas for demos of new Web sites and technologies.

What The Competition Is Doing

Another trend indicator is the activity of your competitors. Check out their sites as often as possible to see what they have done with their content in response to your market challenge. Try to find out where they are advertising, and analyze their banner ad message and design. They may unknowingly help you spot competitive opportunities.

In many industries, a quality site with good potential ends up being bought out by a larger company or is granted a large infusion of venture capital; this happens on a regular basis. I have seen many small, quality sites in different industries, which were in friendly competition with other sites, suddenly bought out and turned overnight into overwhelming competition. You can never be complacent about the apparently sleepy nature of a quality but slow-changing competitive site. One way to prevent surprises is to maintain open lines of communication with friendly competition. You never know when you might want to develop an alliance in response to an even larger competitor—it happens every day.

A Commanding Knowledge of the Technology

In order to be prepared and responsive to trends, you must have more than a passing understanding of what the new technologies are and how they work.

A good example is Java applets, used for animating and rotating ads on your site. Learning about applets may seem like a daunting and impossible task to deal with as a non-programmer; but the more you read, the more you will discover that these technologies can sometimes be "plug and played" right into your HTML code. Check out the Gamelan Web site `http://www.gamelan.com` which lists hundreds of useful Java applications—many of them free. While most require some basic understanding of Java, others can be pasted right into your home page. The same goes for ActiveX and CGI scripts. Most of these programs are low-priced gems that will enable you to set up value added features and services such as discussion forums, chat rooms, guest logs, and others with virtually no programming required.

One benchmark to aim for is to budget ten hours at least once a month to experimenting with—not just reading about—the new technologies. Another time budgeting suggestion is to spend ten hours per month learning how to use graphics programs such as Director, Shockwave, or Corel Photopaint, as well as animation-producing utilities such as GIF Construction Set `http://www.mindworkshop.com`. Visit the Internet Link Exchange `http://www.linkexchange.com` to learn more about designing and testing banner ads.

ADVERTISING AND MARKETING NEWS

Cowles New Media—Media Central
http://www.mediacentral.com/index

1st Step—Web Design and Marketing Daily
http://www.interbiznet.com/ibn/nomad.html

Newslinx—Daily Web News
http://www.newslinx.com

Internet Marketing Communications—Interactive Marketing Magazine
http://www.imcWeb.com/IMM/IMMframz.htm

NlightN—Subscription Magazine Article Research Service
http://www.nlightn.com

Advertising Age
http://www.adage.com

Internet-Sales Digest
http://www.mmgco.com

ZD Net
http://www.zdnet.com

CMP TechWeb
http://www.techWeb.com

IDG Publications
http://www.idg.com

C|net
http://www.cnet.com

Iworld
http://www.iworld.com

Boardwatch Resource Guide
http://www.boardwatch.com

SI Software
http://www.sisoftware.com

Set your goals high: don't just learn how to use the software, actually use it to develop banner ads that can be tested. If you aren't ready to test these banner ads with ad dollars, why not test them on the Link Exchange and the other reciprocal banner exchanges? Finally, you should allocate one hour per day to reviewing news, tips, and articles from the sites listed below. You will be amazed at the commanding knowledge you can gain by being plugged in.

Onsite Promotion

Your success at attracting repeat visitors is as important as attracting first-time visitors, so you need to be creative about promoting your site to them. You might want to offer a free weekly newsletter or regular product updates by e-mail. An occasional contest giveaway that is promoted exclusively to registered users can do wonders for interest in your sales message; the more meaningful the contest offer, the greater mileage you will get out of it through word of mouth. As a way of standing out from the other content, these offers can be presented as exciting banner ads on your own site. Regularly changing the contest will also help generate repeat visits. Some of the most sophisticated contest forms include a "scavenger hunt," where visitors must find clues within the context of many pages on your site. It's a proven way to get them to read the important sections and it can cost very little.

Other options for increasing repeat business include the following: Presenting a limited-time offer available only to registered visitors is a good way to turn lurkers into prospects with known demographics. Targeted e-mail campaigns can produce results of up to 30%. Displaying any "Site Of The Day" or other award banners or favorable comments from visitors, provides ready-made testimonials as to the quality of your site. Experimenting with sound and animation to trumpet new benefits on your site is a sure way to arouse visitors and keep them coming back.

Taking the Plunge

If you intend to test the Web advertising waters, there is no time like the present; the competition and clutter of Web advertising will only grow over time. You can count on major changes occurring in technology and Web advertising vehicles every six months or sooner, but, by following the trends, you can prepare early for any exciting Web advertising prospects that come along.

Check out the sites listed in the Advertising and Marketing News sidebar. Regular monitoring of these sites will put you steps ahead of the competition and keep you abreast of the frequent and inevitable changes in the Web advertising scene.

11

The Benefits of Professional Help

Nothing like the Internet and the World Wide Web has ever existed before. Founded in anarchy, the Net/Web community developed as a group of people who gave their knowledge and creativity freely to others. If you needed help on the Internet, you could almost always find someone willing to give it to you. Now, for better or worse, the marketplace has entered the on-line community, and some knowledge and services cost money; however, the vast majority of information can still be had for free.

But where do you go to get the best information or services? One of the conundrums of the Web is that all the front doors look the same; when searching for on-line help, one usually can't tell just by looking which entrances lead to superior quality and which open on dives that should be quickly passed by. This chapter helps eliminate fruitless searching by giving you directions to the best resources available for promoting your Web site. Not surprisingly, many of the sites and organizations listed here are discussed elsewhere in this book. This chapter provides a handy reference to them, as well as to many additional resources.

Often, areas on the Web and on the Net don't fall into neat subject-based categories; this is true of many of the resources listed here. Where appropriate I have listed them in different places, but look around. For example, some of the sites listed in "Advertising" could easily be under "Marketing," and vice versa. Also, things change so quickly online that I have undoubtedly missed some great resources. To help keep you up to date, I've provided some on-line sources to check for new entries into a variety of fields.

Search Engines

The popular search engines provide an important source of visitors for most sites. Special subject search engines may provide a high percentage of hits, because their users often match your target audience. To help the search engines do their jobs, you must know how they work, submit your URL to them properly, and design your site to score well with them.

Popular Search Engines

I list the popular search engines in what I consider to be the order of their importance to most Web sites. But don't ignore any of them.

Yahoo

Yahoo `http://www.yahoo.com` is the most influential general directory on the Web. Not only is Yahoo popular, but its listings are under human control, which means you may be able to affect how your site is listed. If you aren't already listed, go to `http://add.yahoo.com/bin/add?`. Check `http://www.yahoo.com/docs/info/addfaq.html#detail` for questions you may have about the process.

Alta Vista

Alta Vista `http://www.altavista.digital.com` is one of the most popular and powerful spider indexes. If you aren't in its database, click on the Add URL link `http://www.altavista.digital.com/cgi-bin/query?pg=tmpl&v=addurl.html` at the bottom of any Alta Vista page.

Excite

Excite `http://www.excite.com` includes a large database and uses "Intelligent Concept Extraction" to extract a site's dominant theme. The Add URL link will take you to Excite's submission page `http://www.excite.com/Search/add_url.html?amt`.

InfoSeek Ultra

InfoSeek Ultra `http://ultra.infoseek.com/` represents the next generation in spider indexes. InfoSeek Ultra features fast submission times, a large section of the Web indexed, and quick search times. To submit your URL, click on InfoSeek Ultra's Add URL link `http://ultra.infoseek.com/AddUrl?pg=addurl.html&sv=US&lk=1`.

HotBot

HotBot `http://www.hotbot.com`, HotWired's search engine, features a parallel processing scheme developed for the Inktomi search engine at Berkeley. If HotBot has not found you, you can submit your site directly to HotBot using the Add Url link `http://www.hotbot.com/full/addurl.html`. You only need to add your top page and HotBot will index your entire site.

WebCrawler

WebCrawler `http://www.Webcrawler.com`, a moderately powerful search engine with a relatively small database, was the default search engine for America Online members. Submit your site by clicking on the Add URL link `http://www.Webcrawler.com/WebCrawler/SubmitURLS.html`.

Lycos

Lycos `http://www.lycos.com`, one of the oldest and most eccentric search engines, does not index the full text of a page but instead creates an abstract that incorporates titles, headers, and repeated words and phrases. Lycos also runs a directory. You can submit directly at `http://www.lycos.com/addasite.html`.

Magellan

Magellan `http://www.mckinely.com` is a search engine closely tied to a directory that includes reviews. Magellan provides an Add Site link `http://www.mckinley.com/feature.cgi?add_bd`, but this feature will submit your site for consideration only to the directory, not to the general Web search engine.

Open Text

Open Text Index `http://index.opentext.net/` is maintained as a demonstration of the power of Open Text indexing software. Submit your site at `http://index.opentext.net/main/submitURL.html`. Since Open Text's spider doesn't follow internal links, you will have to individually submit each page you want in their database.

Special Subject Search Engines

It may be difficult to appear on the first page of 22,703 results from an Alta Vista search, but it is easy to show up well on a search engine that specializes in handling sites like yours. Here's how to find the right special subject search engines for you.

100 Specialized Search Engines!

100 Specialized Search Engines! `http://www.Webcom.com/Webscout/Search/Engines.html` provides links to 100 special subject search engines, from women to Japan to sports to Shakespeare.

WebScout Index Page

WebScout Index Page `http://www.Webcom.com/Webscout/Search/Engines.html` provides a list of sites such as 80s Search (an engine that looks for information related to the 1980s), Freedom.co.uk (gay, lesbian, bisexual, and transgender Web sites), and Electric Manufacturers on the Web (links to hardware companies).

Search Engines—Beaucoup!

Search Engines—Beaucoup! `http://www.beaucoup.com/engines.html` links to over 500 search engines categorized by different subjects such as Education, Science and Technology, and Software. A tour de force!

Commercial Sites Index

Commercial Sites Index `http://www.directory.net` was begun at MIT and is now maintained by Open Market as a public service. Lists commercial sites.

Apollo International Advertising

Apollo International Advertising `http://apollo.co.uk/Apollo International Directory` is a fee-based directory of services and articles available world wide on the Web.

Search Engine Function

The Web community is fortunate for the following sites, which provide insights on search engine function. These benefactors should be commended, and you should visit them periodically to see what's new.

Webmaster's Guide: How Search Engines Work

Webmaster's Guide: How Search Engines Work `http://calafia.com/Webmasters/work.htm` is Calafia Consulting's excellent resource on what makes the major search engines tick. Calafia studied each search engine to determine its characteristics and to see if it lived up to its claims. The site is periodically updated.

Search Engine Tutorial

Search Engine Tutorial `http://www.digital-cafe.com/~Webmaster/set01.html` provides tips on how to design your page with the search engines in mind. This site is well conceived and researched and is updated periodically. Another must see.

Search Tools

Search Tools `http://rs.internic.net/scout/toolkit/search.html` outlines the capabilities and characteristics of the major search engines and directories. Brought to you by InterNIC's Scout service.

Meta Tags

Meta tags can work magic with your ranking and description on some search engines.

META Tagging for Search Engines

META Tagging for Search Engines `http://www.stars.com/Search/Meta/Tag.html` discusses how some of the major search engines deal with meta tags. The site does a good job of keeping current with meta tag developments that relate to search engines.

META Tag Builder

META Tag Builder `http://vancouver-Webpages.com/VWbot/mk-metas.html` provides a clever fill in form that will build an HTML header for you, complete with the appropriate meta tags.

Award Sites

Award sites highlight the newest, best, or coolest sites available. These ten Award sites represent a potent sources of visitors—if you're good enough to get listed. New award sites show up every day.

Cool Site of the Day

Cool Site of the Day (CSotD) `http://cool.infi.net/` is generally acknowledged as the originator of the "Cool Site" genre. CSotD is also the source of the Cool Site of the Year awards. To be considered, click the Submit/Help link, or e-mail `cool@infi.net`.

Lycos Top 5% of the Web

The Lycos Top 5% of the Web site `http://point.lycos.com/categories/index.html` is one of the older and more ubiquitous rating services on the Web. If you don't find your site in the database, you can submit it by clicking Add a Site and entering your URL in the field provided. However, this process only adds your site to the Lycos database; Lycos's site reviewers determine which sites get added to the Top 5% list.

Too Cool

Too Cool `http://toocool.com/`, in addition to selecting a daily Too Cool site, is also a vehicle for the Web design services of its staff. To submit your site for review, click on About Too Cool, then click "mail" under "How does Too Cool find the coolest sites every day?"

Project Cool

After Glenn Davis founded Cool Site of the Day and launched the "cool site" genre, he left it to start Project Cool `http://www/projectcool.com/`. In addition to daily Sightings, this site includes Developer Zone (a resource for Web designers) and Future Focus (editorials about the Web, communications, and technology). To submit your site, go to the main page and select Sightings, then click Submit a Sighting from the resulting page.

Starting Point

Starting Point `http://www.stpt.com/` looks as if it's trying to compete with Yahoo by offering a little bit of everything. The Today's Hot site is located at the bottom of the page; if you want to be considered, click the Submit button in the menu bar and fill in the fields provided. The description field is limited to 512 characters.

2ask

The 2ask site `http://www.2ask.com/` ranks its awards on a global scale, using a 5-star judging system. 2ask judges according to speed and ease of use, design, quality of content, timeliness, level of interactivity, and use of technology. To ask 2ask to check you out, go to the main page, click Nominate a Site, then choose from a list of categories that best fits your site. Note that there is also an area where you can review a site, if you'd rather write your own review.

c|net Best of the Web

Megasite c|net's Best of the Web `http://www.cnet.com/Content/Reviews/BestofWeb/index.html` provides a growing collection of sites reviewed by a large team of staff members and freelancers. Submission, however, is only available to c|net members (membership is free). To submit your site, click Submit Your Favorite Web Site and fill out the fields provided. Don't just include your 25-word description in the main field; they're looking for *why* you think the site should be included in their database. Be persuasive.

Cybertown

Cybertown `http://www.cybertown.com/` is an impressive collection of links and resources brought together under a virtual city metaphor. Cybertown currently gets about 4 million hits per month. E-mail your URL to `cybermail@cybertown.com` with a request that the URL be added to the list of considered sites.

Netscape's What's Cool

Probably the most-hit What's Cool site on the Web, Netscape's What's Cool page `http:/home.netscape.com/home/whats-cool.html` has the advantage of being a menu item in Netscape's Navigator browser, which currently controls somewhere from 60–80% of the browser market. Unfortunately, Netscape no longer appears to accept nominations for sites. Instead, sites are reviewed by the faceless "Netscape cool team." You can, however, look into buying advertising for the page under the Web Site Advertising link.

WebCrawler Top 25

WebCrawler's Top 25 list `http://www.Webcrawler.com/WebCrawler/Top25.html` does not provide a way to get your site on the list—unless it becomes wildly popular, in which case it will be included automatically, since WebCrawler's Top 25 lists the sites on the Web that are most frequently linked. The site does, however, offer you an idea of which sites people are visiting; from there you can contact the site owners to inquire about cross-linking your site.

Automatic Submission Services

Often associated with more comprehensive fee-based promotion services, these sites automatically submit your URL. Look at Yahoo's listing of Announcement Services `http://www.yahoo.com/Business_and_Economy/Companies/Internet_Services/Web_Presence_Providers/Announcement_Services` for newcomers to the field. For more comprehensive promotion, see "Professional Publicists," below.

Submit-It

Most Web masters consider Scott Bannister's Submit-It `http://www.submit-it.com` the best of the automatic submission services. Scott has two services, one free and the other paid. The free service submits your site to 15 search engines, announce sites, and directories including Alta Vista, Yahoo, and WebCrawler; the free service also has the smart option of allowing you to decide which of the 15 sites you want to submit to.

PostMaster2

PostMaster2 `http://www.netcreations.com/postmaster/` is primarily a commercial site, with a "try before you buy" option that allows you to post to about 20 main search engines and directories.

Add It!

Add It! `http://www.liquidimaging.com/liqimg/submit/usa/index.html` will send your URL to 30 important sites. Unfortunately, Add It! doesn't allow you to deselect a site from the list.

Promote-It!

Promote-It! `http://www.iTools.com/promote-it/promote-it.html` will make automatic submission to 19 search engines and directories. Promote-It! gives extensive links list of other free sites including cool sites, sites of the day, specialized sites, commercial sites, and so on.

Announce Sites

These sites and newsgroups act as venues for getting the word out on what's new on the Web.

What's New Too

The widely read What's New Too `http://newtoo.manifest.com` lists over 500 new Web sites a day. Visit and submit your new site.

Netsurfer Digest

Netsurfer Digest `http://www.netsurf.com/nsd/` is a weekly e-mail newsletter detailing new and interesting news, places, and resources online. Each issue is e-mailed in either text-only or HTML format and includes brief summaries and descriptions of the featured sites.

announce.net

Announce.net `http://www.announcenet.com/` offers direct links to 35 What's New pages, including regulars like Yahoo! and Alta Vista as well as less common sites like What's New in Japan, New WAIS Resources, and New Spots to Shop.

Global Internet's NetHappenings

The Global Internet's NetHappenings site `http://www.mid.net/NET/` not only lets you submit your site information to its daily listing of new and interesting sites, it also includes the ability to search articles by title, keyword, and subject.

The Green Eggs Report

The Green Eggs Report `http://ibd.ar.com/ger/` takes an unusual approach to collecting URLs. The Green Eggs' Rumor Database System perches on the edge of the Usenet spool, grabbing URLs from messages that are posted to newsgroups. To link your site to this directory, just post a message containing your URL to a newsgroup.

comp.infosystems.www.announce

The Usenet newsgroup `comp.infosystems.www.announce` is a moderated group that posts messages about new Web resources, sites, and site changes. Check it out and post a message about your site.

Nerd World What's New

Although its name suggests a wealth of computer geek-related items, Nerd World `http://www.nerdworld.com/whatsnew.html` is actually a fairly large subject index and search engine that receives over one million views per month.

Hundreds of Links

Many sites exist just to provide links to hundreds of other sites that will link to you. Most of these "links to links" take you directly to the submission page.

The Internet Promotions Megalist

The Internet Promotions Megalist `http://www.2020tech.com/submit.html` includes links to What's New services, search engines, Usenet newsgroups, Web sites that require reciprocal links, and an array of specialized sites ranging from Africa-related to Women-specific sites. To help you out, the creators of the Megalist have marked "very important Internet resources" with stars.

Starting Points

Starting Points `http://dfrontier.com/starting_pts.html`, a public service from i-frontier, provides links to the submission forms of over 100 popular sites where you can submit your URL.

A1 Directory

A1 Directory `http://www.a1co.com/index.html` provides links to over 630 sites where you can promote or link your Web site for free. Indexed by category, A1 Directory recommends you start by investigating the potential links for the category closest to you. An enormous list and great resource.

WebStep Top 100

WebStep `http://www.mmgco.com/top100.html` offers 100 free sites and search engines to which you can submit your information, with a short description of each to help you choose which ones will benefit the most from your announcement. The list is updated frequently, so check back when you're out surfing to ensure that your links got placed.

Go Net-Wide

Organized alphabetically, Go Net-Wide `http://www.shout.net/~whitney/html/gopublic.html` provides links to over 100 sites, including unusual ones like Sherlock Holmes Links, The URL Centrifuge, and several variations of cybermalls.

InfoSpace

InfoSpace `http://www.infospace.com/`, a relative newcomer to the Web, offers worldwide telephone directories, business directories, government "blue pages," fax numbers, and more.

Freelinks

Freelinks `http://www.freelinks.com` provides a categorized links list of databases, search engines, and links pages where you can list your site for free.

Web Books and Magazines

Here's a grab bag of some important Internet-related books and magazines. New ones appear every day, so don't be a stranger to your bookstore or sites like Amazon `http://www.amazon.com`. You can also keep current by checking Yahoo's listing of Internet-related magazines `http://www.yahoo.com/Business_and_Economy/Products_and_Services/Magazines/Computers/Internet/`.

Internet World

Internet World `http://www.iw.com`, an established authoritative magazine for Internet users, includes Web sites in some of its stories. Visit *Internet World*'s Press Release Page at `http://www.iw.com/pr/index.shtml`; then, if you've read the magazine and just know they need to publish your URL, try contacting Senior Editor Andrew Kantor `ak@iw.com`. If you feel the Surfboard section needs your site, contact Eric Berlin or Andrew Kantor at `surf@iw.com`.

NetGuide

NetGuide `http://techWeb.cmp.com/ng/home/main/` covers the full spectrum of Web issues, from HTML tips to financial sites to modems. Press releases can be sent to `pressrel@netguide.cmp.com`. If you feel you should be listed in *NetGuide*'s Maximum Impact section, try contacting one of the senior editors, Judith H. Bernstein `jbernste@cmp.com` or Kate Gerwig `kgerwig@cmp.com`, or Associate Editor Kathleen Sands `ksands@cmp.com`.

Yahoo! Internet Life

You can hardly turn a page of *Yahoo! Internet Life* `http://www.yil.com` without tripping over a passel of URLs. Send new site announcements to Editorial Assistant Elissa Klotz `elissa_klotz@zd.com`. Alternately, browse through the magazine, see which columnist might be interested in your site, and send that person a note. The staff list is available at `http://www.zdnet.com/yil/content/misc/staff.html`. If you still can't determine who to target, try Senior Editor Elisabeth Holzer `eholzer@zd.com`.

Wired

Wired http://www.hotwired.com/wired, the premier magazine covering the Internet, sprinkles a few URLs in its feature articles, but the nuggets increase substantially in the Street Cred and Net Surf sections.

Street Cred singles out notable books, music, and Web sites for capsule reviews. Where appropriate, Street Cred lists a URL at the bottom of an article. If you want to be considered for inclusion in Street Cred, send your press release or other submission material to streetcred@wired.com.

Net Surf (which usually follows Street Cred) includes a jumble of sites and Web explorations, sometimes loosely tied together by a common theme. Featured sites have a short review.

New Riders' Official World Wide Web Yellow Pages

New Riders' Official World Wide Web Yellow Pages (aka *NROWWWYP*) represents the annual print and CD version of the popular Web site http://www.mcp.com/nrp/wwwyp. To submit your site to *NROWWWYP*, go to http://www.mcp.com/nrp/wwwyp/submit.html and fill out the form. You will be included in the on-line version for sure and most likely included in the print and CD version as well, although the editors don't guarantee it.

Que's Mega Web Directory

Que's Mega Web Directory yearly directory lists over 18,000 sites on over 1,000 pages. The information is also listed on the included CD in a searchable form that features hotlinks to the Web. The book and CD are alphabetically organized by topic. You can submit your URL for inclusion in the next version to either Dean J. Rositano or Robert A. Rositano at info@simply.com.

Walking the World Wide Web

Walking the World Wide Web includes over 750 pages, most of them listings of Web sites. Author Shannon T. Settle's Web-savvy approach helps the reader surf the Web efficiently and productively. To submit your site to *Walking the World Wide Web*, go to http://www.vmedia.com/vvc/onlcomp/wwww2nd/recommend.html and fill out the form. Or send the information directly to author Shannon T. Settle at shannon@vmedia.com.

E-Zines

E-zines can be a great source of free publicity. Here I list some of the more popular e-zines, as well as directories that can help you find e-zines that cover the subject material of your site.

HotWired

HotWired `http://www.hotwired.com/` began as an on-line cousin to Wired magazine, but it soon morphed into its own entity, sharing only its attitude, influence, and part of its name with *Wired*. The Net Surf Central section spotlights Web sites and offers brief commentary on a daily basis. E-mail editor June Cohen `hotsurf@hotwired.com` to submit your site for review.

NetGuide Live

Like HotWired, NetGuide Live `http://www.netguide.com/gen/page/Home` is an on-line magazine that has ties with a print publication, in this case, *NetGuide*. However, NetGuide Live is not the same site as the Web version of *NetGuide*. The SiteGeist section lists new sites and spotlights; NetGuide Live's Best of the Web lists their picks for top sites in a dozen categories, with over 50,000 sites rated and reviewed. Submit your new site's URL to `newsites@netguide.com`; also e-mail The List Guy `listguy@netguide.com`, who groups and presents new sites into subjects.

e-zine-list

The e-zine-list `http://www.meer.net/johnl/e-zine-list` provides a directory of over 1,300 electronic magazines and newsletters that are accessible through the Internet and other services. Check to see which e-zines should be writing about you.

Todd Kuipers' E-mail-Zines-List

Todd Kuipers' E-mail-Zines-List `http://www.merak.com/~tkuipers/elists/elists.htm` lists hundreds of 'zines mailed directly to the subscriber, categorized by subject. Search through and then contact the 'zines that may be interested in writing about your site.

Newsgroups and Mailing Lists

Newsgroups and mailing lists can provide invaluable places to promote your site. But first you must find the right group, and then you must approach it correctly. For information on newsgroups you can try to find either the group's charter or its FAQ (Frequently Asked/Answered Questions). Both are periodically posted in many newsgroups, but you can also search for FAQs at `http://www.cis.ohio-state.edu/hypertext/faq/usenet/top.html`. Some newsgroups will not have this information available.

I include the best mailing list and newsgroup search tools below. For other mailing list directories and more information about mailing lists, check out Yahoo `http://www.yahoo.com/Computers_and_Internet/Internet/Mailing_Lists`.

Reference.COM

Reference.COM `http://www.reference.com` principally acts as a giant archive of messages from publicly accessible mailing lists and newsgroups. The archive provides sophisticated search tools to help you quickly hone in on messages in various discussion groups. But besides searching for messages, Reference.COM also includes the capability of searching for particular mailing lists or newsgroups themselves.

Liszt

Liszt `http://www.liszt.com` is to mailing lists what a spider index search engine is to the Web. Liszt uses a spider that checks servers to see if they host mailing lists, and, if so, Liszt collects information on the mailing list in the Liszt database. Mailing lists can also be added directly to Liszt, if the spider hasn't picked them up in its travels.

PAML

PAML (Publicly Accessible Mailing Lists) `http://www.neosoft.com/internet/paml` may not have the largest database nor the sexiest of interfaces, but it presents the most personal approach of these directories, so it is worth a mention here. You can search for mailing lists by name or subject keyword.

CataList

CataList `http://www.lsoft.com/lists/listref.html` is maintained by L-Soft, the producer of the LISTSERV software that manages mailing lists. You can use CataList to search for publicly accessible mailing LISTSERV lists. This service sometimes contains mailing lists missed by the others.

Deja News

Deja News `http://www.dejanews.com` bills itself as "The Source for Internet Newsgroups!", and it isn't far off base. Deja News collects over 500 megabytes of new messages each day and lets you search through them. Great for finding the right newsgroup to post in.

The Reporter's Guide To Internet Mailing Lists

The Reporter's Guide To Internet Mailing Lists, by Timothy Broeker `http://www.daily.umn.edu/~broeker/guide.html`, takes a look at how mailing lists can make a journalist's life more productive.

Newsgroup Self Search

Most software that accesses Usenet newsgroups offers the capability of searching through a list of all the newsgroups subscribed to by your site. You may have to search for abbreviations or variations on keywords—and you may have to get creative in keyword selection—but you can usually find most of the appropriate sites very easily yourself.

Advertising

These resources will help you get your ad up and running. Be sure to commit Chapters 8, 9, and 10 to memory before spending any money!

Web Ad Rate Guide

SI Software's Web Ad Rate Guide `http://www.sisoftware.com/sirate1.htm` charts advertising rates on search engines, award sites, popular sites, and magazines. The guide also includes heavy annotations and gives insights on discounts. A terrific resource for the Web site advertiser.

Advertising Age

Advertising Age `http://www.adage.com`, an on-line newspaper, is all about marketing and advertising on the Web. Advertising Age provides daily news, links, resources, and archives. Check it out.

The Internet Advertising Resource Guide

The Internet Advertising Resource Guide `http://pilot.msu.edu/unit/adv/internet-advertising-guide.htm`, maintained by Dr. Hairong Li at Michigan State University, features a multitude of links on all aspects of advertising on the Net.

Inet Marketing Database

Inet Marketing Database `http://www.envision.net/marketing/inet/inetdata1.html` provides rated, annotated links to sites that take advertising.

Internet Link Exchange

Internet Link Exchange `http://www.linkexchange.com/` is the primary exchange company operating on the Web. ILE provides up-to-the-minute statistics on visits, click-throughs, the number of times a banner is displayed, and a display-to-click ratio. If you don't have a banner, or want to make sure you're designing them effectively, free banner creation services are also available.

Advertising on Usenet—How to Do It

Advertising on Usenet—How to Do It, by Joel K. Furr in the newsgroup `news.announce.newusers` (or on the Web at `http://www.danger.com/advo.html`), provides a low-key, common-sense approach to advertising on the Usenet from someone with experience and insight.

Advertising in Cyberspace

Advertising in Cyberspace `http://www.cnh.mv.com/ipusers/cv/cyber.html` has, in their own words, "the objective of providing the latest information related to advertising on the World Wide Web." This site includes resources, tools, advertising innovations, and a cool site of the week.

Marketing

Marketers have embraced the Web from the moment it was commercialized. Here's some of the best of their resources.

Internet Sales Discussion List

The Internet Sales Discussion List is a mailing list on Internet sales, marketing, and Web commerce. Lurk for a while and read the wisdom. You can join by filling out the form at `http://www.mmgco.com/isales.html`.

Kim Bayne's Marketing Lists on the Internet

Kim Bayne's Marketing Lists on the Internet `http://www.bayne.com/wolfBayne/htmarcom/mktglist.html` gives links to over 90 marketing-related Internet resources. The links are mostly to mailing lists, but they also include newsgroups and Web sites.

Internet Marketing Discussion List Archives

Internet Marketing Discussion List Archives `http://www.i-m.com/` contains the records of the now-defunct, legendary mailing list on Internet marketing. In July of 1994, when Glenn Fleishman told me he was going to start this list, I merely grunted. However, Glenn's vision and dedication have proven themselves in the quality of the list and the relevancy of its archives

1st Steps—Marketing and Design Daily

1st Steps—Marketing and Design Daily `http://www.interbiznet.com/ibn/nomad.html` is an authoritative newsletter covering all aspects of marketing on the Internet. The site includes archives to look up past features.

Inet Marketing Report

Inet Marketing Report `http://www.envision.net/marketing/inet/` provides information to businesses that want to make profitable use of the Internet.

Publicity

Get the word out for free using these publicity resources, which include news services and sites dedicated to helping you promote your URL.

Media Central

Updated daily, the Media Central `http://www.mediacentral.com/` news service covers all realms of communications, from broadcast and cable to interactive media. Contact Marc Perton, Editor-in-Chief `mperton@mediacentral.com`; Larry Jaffee, Managing Editor `ljaffee@mediacentral.com`; or Frances Katz, Associate Editor `fkatz@mediacentral.com`.

Newsbytes

Covering all aspects of the telecommunications, computer, and on-line worlds, Newsbytes `http://www.newsbytes.com/` delivers news releases and data via either their Web site or e-mail subscription. Contact Wendy Woods, Editor `Wendy_Woods@newsbytes.com`.

Website Promoters Resource Center

Website Promoters Resource Center `http://www.wprc.com/` is a resource of links and information about a wide range of subjects of interest to the Web site promoter. The site includes information on banner and link exchanges, links to articles and other documents, on-line press contacts, and more.

Resources & Software for Web Advertising, Marketing, PR, and E-mail

SI Software's Resources & Software for Web Advertising, Marketing, PR, and E-mail `http://www.sisoftware.com` provides a number of resources for publicity and advertising, including links and capsule reviews to over 400 promotion resources. Also see "Advertising" for their Web Ad Rate Guide.

Professional Publicists

The importance of Web site promotion becomes clear when one looks at the enormous numbers of people have made it their business to tout Web sites. In this section I list some of the more important services, but rest assured that there are many more available that will do a top-notch job.

The Ward Group

Eric Ward, the vision behind the Ward Group `http://www.netpost.com`, ranks as one of the pioneers of marketing on the World Wide Web. Eric, the grandfather of Web site promotion, offers two distinct services, NetPOST and Eric Ward's URL Wire.

NetPOST identifies and individually submits to a collection of resources, from key search engines to Web news services to Web TV and Web radio shows. Eric Ward's URL Wire sends "news about Web sites and Web events to the exact people that cover such Web news and Web events, in 10 countries."

Multimedia Marketing Group

Multimedia Marketing Group `http://www.mmgco.com` is a promotions and public relations services that states, "Successful promotion of a Web site is a matter of a continuing effort that includes hard work, knowledge and experience, effective tools, and contacts in the on-line community. There are no shortcuts, and there is no magic potion." Multimedia Marketing Group provides both free and fee-based services for building Web site traffic.

WPRC Web Site Promotion Services

WPRC Web Site Promotion Services `http://www.wprc.com/wwpc/wprcwwpc.shtml` offers a range of services, from submission of URLs to search engines and directories to media and advertising placement, to complete management of a Web promotion campaign.

Netiquette

An understanding of netiquette is essential if you want to succeed in the on-line world. The basic premise of netiquette is that on-line discussions involve communication with humans, so treat them humanely. Here are some netiquette resources.

The Net: User Guidelines and Netiquette

A good foundation in netiquette can be gleaned from The Net: User Guidelines and Netiquette by Arlene H. Rinaldi `http://rs6000.adm.fau.edu/rinaldi/netiquette.html`.

Primer on How to Work With the Usenet Community

The "Primer on How to Work With the Usenet Community" by Chuq Von Rospach in the newsgroup `news.misc` or at the Web site `http://www01.ny.us.ibm.net/userinfo/uuprimer.html` provides a great background in proper newsgroup behavior.

INDEX

F

G

H

I

J

K

L

T

U

W

More from Peachpit Press

25 Steps to Safe Computing

Don Sellers

With planning, many computer-related health problems can be avoided. *25 Steps to Safe Computing* tells you how to reduce your risk with well-illustrated, easy-to-follow advice. It contains ergonomic tips on setting up work areas, as well as chapters on backache, headache, tendinitis, radiation, pregnancy, kid's concerns, and much more. *$5.95 (72 pages)*

America Online 3 for Macintosh: Visual QuickStart Guide

Maria Langer

–AND–

America Online 3 for Windows 95: Visual QuickStart Guide

Maria Langer

With over 6 million members, America Online is the world's largest online service provider. Both Visual QuickStart Guides provide an easy, step-by-step guide for beginners to getting up and running with AOL and for intermediate users to gain more in depth understanding of the service. These books help readers go from installing the newest version of the software to exchanging e-mail, using newsgroups and the Web browser, and participating in forums and live chats. Key America Online areas, such as Entertainment, NewsStand, Computers and Software, Market-place, and Kids Only, are described and illustrated, and appendices offer lists of shortcut keys, forums, and companies.
Macintosh: $16.95 (304 pages)
Windows 95: $17.95 (288 pages w/ disk)

A Blip in the continuum, Macintosh Edition (Includes Disk)

Robin Williams and John Tollett

–AND–

A Blip in the continuum, Windows Edition (Includes Disk)

Robin Williams and John Tollett

In this full-color book, author Robin Williams and illustrator John Tollett celebrate the new wave of type design known as "grunge" typography. The book consists of famous and not-so-famous quotes about type and design set in a range of grunge fonts, using rule-breaking layouts. The illustrations, created in Fractal Design Painter, complement the text. Includes a companion disk with 21 of the best freeware and shareware grunge fonts, several of which were newly created for this book. *Both versions are $22.95 (96 pages w/ disk)*

CHAT

Nan McCarthy

CHAT is a fast-moving, compelling story of online romance that will appeal to all cyberjunkies and anyone looking for an entertaining story. Bev, a tough-minded book editor, cautiously begins corresponding with Maximilian, a flamboyant copywriter who approaches her after seeing her messages in an online writers forum. Their relationship gradually becomes more intense and their e-mails less inhibited as the story unfolds entirely through their messages to one another. *$7.95 (136 pages)*

Dan Gookin's Web Wambooli

Dan Gookin

Not just "another Internet book," this one showcases the perspective and experience of a computer book guru. A non-technical, jargon-limited handbook that's as entertaining as it is useful, it covers the most interesting, fun, and valuable aspects of the Internet and the World Wide Web. Covers hardware and software; choosing a service provider; using Netscape; accessing newsgroups; games, entertainment, and chat sites; and what's ahead and how to keep up. *$22.95 (400 pages)*

Director Multimedia Studio Authorized

Macromedia, Inc.

–AND–

Lingo Authorized

Macromedia, Inc.

Developed by Macromedia's staff and user-tested in Macromedia's Authorized Training Centers, these large-format books include the complete curricula from the Training Centers' multi-day hands-on courses on Director 5. Master teachers present lessons in manageable step-by-step worksessions, letting you work through the courses at your own pace. The cross-platform CD-ROMs contain practice files of all lessons and demo versions of the Macromedia programs. With these Authorized books, you'll master the basics of Director in only 40 hours of hands-on training.

Director Multimedia Studio Authorized (Level 1):
$39.95 (264 pages w/ CD-ROM)

Lingo Authorized (Level 2):
$39.95 (288 pages w/ CD-ROM)

Home Sweet Home Page and the Kitchen Sink

Robin Williams with Dave Mark

This exciting new book/CD-ROM combo provides all the tools you need to get online and create Web pages. *Home Sweet Home Page and the Kitchen Sink* takes a friendly, non-technical approach to planning and designing interactive Web pages with easy-to-follow instructions and delightful illustrations. The CD-ROM provides everything else you need to finish creating your pages, including connection software for AOL, CompuServe, and AT&T. *$24.95 (208 pages)*

HTML for the World Wide Web, 2nd Edition

Elizabeth Castro

This step-by-step guide on using Hypertext Markup Language to design pages for the World Wide Web presumes no prior knowledge of HTML, or even the Internet. It uses clear, concise instructions for creating each element of a Web page. Expanded coverage in this edition includes such major new topics as style sheets and frames, progressive JPEG images and animated GIFs, font and column width controls. *$17.95 (240 pages)*

Internet Explorer 3 for Windows 95/NT: Visual QuickStart Guide

Steven Schwartz

This book is for anyone who wants or needs to browse the World Wide Web. This hands-on guide takes a straightforward, visual approach that enables even those with little past browsing experience to get up and running quickly. New Microsoft Internet Explorer users will find the step-by-step instructions easy to follow and fun, and readers with some Microsoft Internet Explorer experience will benefit from the explanations of important new features with particular emphasis on using new plug-ins such as ActiveX and JavaScript. *$16.95 (208 pages)*

JavaScript for the World Wide Web

Ted Gesing and Jeremy Schneider

JavaScript is a programming language designed to be used in conjunction with HTML, making HTML more powerful and interactive. All predictions are that JavaScript will become as important as HTML, and it is now fully supported in Netscape Navigator 3 and Microsoft Internet Explorer. While other JavaScript books are intended for experienced programmers, this one is for the vast majority of HTML coders who are less technically sophisticated but still would like a useful introduction and handy reference. *$17.95 (220 pages)*

The Little PC Book, 2nd Edition: A Gentle Introduction to Personal Computers

Lawrence J. Magid with Kay Yarborough Nelson

Wouldn't you love having a knowledgeable, witty, endlessly patient pal to coach you through buying and using a PC? Well, you do. Popular columnist and broadcaster Larry Magid's expertise is yours in *The Little PC Book,* described by *The Wall Street Journal* as "the class of the field." This edition includes the latest on Windows 95, the Internet, CD-ROMs, and more. Includes a handy Windows 95 Cookbook section. *$18.95 (384 pages)*

The Little Windows 95 Book

Kay Yarborough Nelson

Your guide to Windows 95. This easy, informative, and entertaining volume spotlights the essentials so you can get to work quickly. Short, fully-illustrated chapters explore the Windows interface in detail, offering tips and tricks the manual doesn't. Each chapter includes a handy summary chart of keyboard shortcuts and quick tips. *$12.95 (144 pages)*

The Macintosh Bible, 6th Edition

Jeremy Judson, Editor

With over 1,000,000 copies in print, the Macintosh reference book that started it all celebrates its tenth anniversary by offering up-to-the-minute information on topics such as fonts, word processing, spreadsheets, graphics, and desktop publishing. *The Macintosh Bible, 6th Edition* tackles every subject area with a clear vision of what Macintosh users need to know in an engaging, no-nonsense style. New sections include the Internet—getting connected, sending email, surfing the Web, and downloading files; troubleshooting—revised and expanded, including details on error message codes; and Home Offices—using your Mac at home for fun and profit *$29.95 (992 pages)*

Netscape 3 for Macintosh: Visual QuickStart Guide

Elizabeth Castro

–AND–

Netscape 3 for Windows: Visual QuickStart Guide

Elizabeth Castro

This book is the perfect introduction to the latest version of Netscape, the most widely used browser of the World Wide Web. You'll learn how to transfer files, read and send e-mail, use the address book, and post to newsgroups. Additionally, the book covers Netscape Gold, with helpful information on how to format your own Web page.
Macintosh: $16.95 (208 pages)
Windows: $16.95 (288 pages)

The PC Bible, Second Edition

Eric Knorr

The PC universe is expanding, and the second edition of *The PC Bible* has grown along with it. Sixteen industry experts collaborated on this definitive guide to PCs, now updated to include Windows 95 and Internet access. Beginning and advanced users will benefit from this book's clear, entertaining coverage of fonts, word processing, spreadsheets, graphics, desktop publishing, databases, communications, utilities, multimedia, games, and more. Winner of a 1994 Computer Press Award. *$29.95 (1000 pages)*

PageMill 2 for Macintosh: Visual QuickStart Guide

Maria Langer

–AND–

PageMill 2 for Windows: Visual QuickStart Guide

Maria Langer

These Visual QuickStart Guides are richly illustrated, step-by-step guides to using all the features of PageMill. As with all books in Peachpit's highly successful Visual QuickStart series (with more than a million copies in print), information is presented in a graphic, visual fashion, with hundreds of screenshots accompanied by clear instructions and loads of helpful tips. *Both versions are $15.95 (184 pages)*

Real World QuarkImmedia

David Blatner

QuarkImmedia is a new product which enables designers to create interactive presentations while working in the familiar XPress environment. *Real World QuarkImmedia* covers making the transition from press to multimedia, building an infrastructure, buttons and menus, animations, sound, QuickTime, building scripts, and exporting projects (including how to export to the Web). The accompanying CD-ROM includes sample Immedia projects, the entire book in Immedia format, and many of the essential ingredients people need to create their own multimedia projects, including buttons, background art, sounds, animations, clip art, and software to help in publishing for the Internet and on CD-ROMs. *$39.95 (464 pages w/ CD-ROM)*

The Painter 4 Wow! Book

Cher Threinen-Pendarvis

Fractal Design Painter has so many features even power users don't know all the tricks. Whatever your skill level, you'll scurry to the computer to try out the examples in *The Painter 4 Wow! Book.* This full-color volume uses hundreds of stunning, original illustrations depicting Painter's full range of styles and effects. Step-by-step descriptions clearly explain how each piece was created by well-known artists, designers, and multimedia producers. *$44.95 (264 pages w/CD-ROM)*

Shocking the Web, Macintosh Edition

Cathy Clarke, Lee Swearingen, and David K. Anderson

–AND–

Shocking the Web, Windows Edition

Cathy Clarke, Lee Swearingen, and David K. Anderson

Shocking the Web is an authoritative hands-on guide by the creators of Macromedia's original Shockwave Web site that shows Director developers how to create high impact, low-bandwidth movies for the Internet. *Shocking the Web* uses detailed case studies and step-by-step design examples throughout to guide developers in creating multimedia content within the Internet's bandwidth limitations. The authors reveal Lingo tips, tricks, and secrets and cover integration of Shockwave with Java. The CD-ROM includes the case studies and design examples, as well as tutorials, template files, setup software, a save-disabled version of Director, and Shockwave clip media for Internet development. *Both versions are $44.95 (464 pages)*

Web Graphics Tools and Techniques

Peter Kentie

This full-color book is an indispensable resource for web site creators needing to master a variety of authoring and graphics tools. It begins with basic web concepts, then proceeds into the specifics of formatting graphics, text, and tables with HTML. Next, it moves deeper into graphics techniques, explaining the use of such tools as Photoshop, Painter, Poser, KPT Welder, GIF Construction Set, and Director. Also covers advanced issues such as tables, clickable maps, 3-D images, and user interaction. *$39.95 (320 pages)*

What's on the Internet, 3rd Edition
Eric Gagnon

This new edition is bigger and better than ever, with entirely updated reviews and a greatly expanded business section. *What's on the Internet* provides an informative, fun, and useful way to find out what online discussion and information groups exist on the Internet and how to connect with them. There are mini-reviews of 2,300 of the most popular newsgroups, a bonanza of Frequently Asked Question (FAQ) files, a 5,500-word subject index, and a list of more than 8,000 Internet newsgroups. *$19.95 (440 pages)*

The Windows 95 Bible

Fred Davis

Here's absolutely everything you need to know about Windows 95, from installation and interface design to telecommunications and multimedia. This fun-to-read, easy-to-use reference is packed with detailed illustrations, plus insider tips and tricks. Reviewing the previous edition, *The New York Times* wrote, "Toss out the other Windows books. This one is the best." (Finalist, Computer Press Awards). *$29.95 (680 pages)*

For online information about these and other Peachpit books and CD-ROMs—plus excerpts from our latest titles—visit our Web site:

Order Form

USA 800-283-9444 • 510-548-4393 • fax 510-548-5991
Canada 800-387-8028 • 416-447-1779 • fax 800-456-0536 or 416-443-0948
http://www.peachpit.com

Qty	Title	Price	Total
	Subtotal		
	Add Applicable Sales Tax*		
	Shipping		
	TOTAL		

Shipping is by UPS ground: $4 for first item, $1 each add'l.

*We are required to pay sales tax in all states with the exceptions of AK, DE, MT, NH, and OR. Please include appropriate sales tax if you live in any state not mentioned above.

Customer Information

Name

Company

Street Address

City State Zip

Phone ( ) Fax ( )
[Required for credit card orders]

Payment Method

❑ Check enclosed ❑ VISA ❑ MasterCard ❑ AMEX

Credit Card # Exp. date

Company Purchase Order #

Tell Us What You Think

Please tell us what you thought of this book: Title: ____________________

What other books would you like us to publish?

PC / MAC

PEACHPIT PRESS • 2414 Sixth Street • Berkeley, CA 94710